Eighteenth-Century
FRANCE

Eighteenth-Century
FRANCE

Six Essays

FREDERICK C. GREEN

Professor Emeritus of French Literature
University of Edinburgh

FREDERICK UNGAR PUBLISHING CO.
NEW YORK

Republished 1964
with some changes by the author

By arrangement with J. M. Dent & Sons Ltd.

First published 1929

Printed in the United States of America

Library of Congress Catalog Card No. 64-21609

FOREWORD

In preparing these essays my aim has been to leave
in the reader's mind a fairly comprehensive picture
of the literary, social, and economic movements
active in eighteenth-century France. Each essay
subject has been chosen with this general purpose
in mind. Where I have gone into backwaters it
has only been to secure a better view of the main
stream.

Many of the facts set forth here are doubtless well
known to specialists in the period: others, I venture
to say, may not yet have been related. In collecting
material I have followed the general plan of going
direct to eighteenth-century sources, both manuscript and printed, although I have taken the liberty
of omitting the customary array of footnotes. The
essay on Voltaire was almost finished when I came
upon M. Cornou's excellent work on Fréron, but I
gladly seize the opportunity of expressing my thanks
to that patient and gifted scholar for several facts
with which I was not previously acquainted.

F. C. G.

June 1928.

CONTENTS

JOHN LAW

In the closing days of December, seventeen hundred and twenty, a post-chaise, emblazoned with the arms of Philip duc de Orleans and Regent of France, jolted its way through the gathering dusk towards Valenciennes en route for Brussels. To the elder of its two occupants at least this bleak, flat, and sodden countryside of northern France, with its sparse pollarded willows and straight, restless poplars, was a welcome sight even to one who had just left behind him the wooded snugness of the fertile Ile de France. This middle-aged, rather tired man was John Law of Lauriston, late Comptroller-General of the Finances of Louis XV of France and adviser to His Majesty in all his councils. The other traveller, not much more than a boy, was his son.

It is true that the carriage which was bearing these two towards Brussels had been sent by order of the Regent or, to be strictly accurate, by the kind offices of the Regent's titular mistress, Mme de Prie. It is also a fact that Law's passports were in perfect order and signed with the boyish scrawl of the young King himself. Still, John Law of Lauriston, of Guermande, and half a dozen other French estates might have been excused a certain uneasiness as he peered out through the streaming windows of the coach. For this Scottish financier carried in his ears the roars of execration of a populace and the lamentations of a ruined and starving nation which but a few months before had hailed him as the saviour of France.

At Valenciennes fresh horses are procured and the chaise sets off again, only to be halted sharply by Monsieur d'Argenson, Intendant to the King at Maubeuge and the son of Law's most implacable enemy, the ex-Keeper of the Seals, now slowly dying at the Convent of Tresnel at Paris. This might be called a dramatic meeting. The greatest gambler in Europe is arrested in headlong flight by the son of a man whose career he had smashed after a three-year duel of wits. Imagine the forty-eight hours that follow, hours of anxious heart-searching on the part of Law who asks himself whether the Regent has played him false, whilst the younger d'Argenson savours with delight the spectacle of the financier's misgivings. But a peremptory order arrives from the Regent to allow Law to proceed unmolested. Of what really happened during those two fateful days we know little. D'Argenson of course records in his diary that Law was badly frightened; but from what we know of the Scotsman's character this is mere guesswork on the part of the over-zealous Intendant. Frightened Law probably was; but if we believe what more impartial enemies have said of his amazing sang-froid, it is practically certain that he did not make d'Argenson a witness of his emotions.

To understand the *dénouement* we must go back to the opening scenes of the astonishing history of John Law. Born in Edinburgh in April 1671, he was the son of a goldsmith who, like most of his colleagues, made much more money by usury than by the practice of his nominal trade. Law's mother, it is said, was descended from the ducal family of Argyll and his political relations with that house lend probability to the story. His father's death left him master of two small estates, Randleston and Lauriston, of a decent fortune, and a very considerable knowledge of finance. In 1694 we find him in London gambling, making love, and studying the credit system of the newly founded Bank of England. Either his luck at cards or his gallantries, or more probably both, embroiled him with a man called Beau Wilson whom he unfortunately killed in a duel, for which he was sent to the Tower. Acquitted of murder, a verdict against which the Wilson family vehemently appealed, Law found it advisable to slip over to Amsterdam where he attached himself to the British Resident and perfected those financial schemes which he had been hatching for some time. The fruits of his studies were offered in the following year to the Scottish Government in the shape of a memorial entitled "Considerations on Currency and Commerce," in which he formulated a plan for the establishment of a great territorial bank. The Argyll clique supported the proposition which was, however, rejected by the canny

Scottish members who were just recovering from the shock of the failure of the Darien scheme. The moment, indeed, was not a propitious one for empiricists. Besides, was not Law a Scotsman and regarded by his fellow-countrymen with the proverbial suspicion accorded to the prophet who preaches his doctrines in his own market-place?

For eight years Law wandered over the Continent, gaming and studying the banking methods of the great Italian, Swiss, German, and Dutch centres. So notorious became his luck at cards that he was frequently invited by the police of these countries to abridge his sojourn. But gambling was for Law merely a pastime. His dream was to be given an opportunity of putting into practice his scheme for the establishment of a great bank built up on subscribed capital and issuing its own notes; in fact, a bank in the modern sense of the term but with the State as its chief shareholder. Law approached Victor Amadeus, King of Sardinia, whom he tried to interest in the plan, but Victor replied brutally that he was not wealthy enough to stand bankruptcy.

In 1708 Law appeared in Paris and almost at once became a brilliant figure in the most exclusive and most vicious society in Europe. "Tall, well-built, of handsome appearance and agreeable manners," says that arch-snob and most exigent of critics, the duc de Saint-Simon, John Law dazzled even the courtiers by his reckless play and extraordinary success with women. Night after night crowds of fashionables, amongst them some princes of the blood, thronged

the residence of the famous tragedienne Mademoiselle
Duclos who maintained one of the most notorious
gaming-houses of the period. Here the imperturbable
Scot ran a faro bank on such a scale that he was
obliged to strike private counters, worth eighteen
louis each, to save himself the trouble of carting his
gold to the rooms. But Duclos's was by no means
his only haunt: for he could be seen, a sack of gold
in each hand, entering Poisson's in the rue Dauphine
or the Hôtel de Gesvres in the rue des Poulies.

As always, however, gambling was for Law a mere
distraction and not an occupation. He had never
renounced his scheme for founding a State bank, and
France seemed at this period a most promising field
for the vast operations seething in the Scotsman's
fertile mind. A few conversations with the duc de
Orleans convinced the future Regent that here
was the one man in Europe who could save France
from the bankruptcy into which she was surely
drifting, thanks to the prodigalities of her old Sultan,
Louis XIV. The Duke introduced Law to Des-
marets, the Minister of Finance, who was enchanted
not only by the novelty of the enterprises outlined
by the brilliant young financier but also by the per-
suasiveness and lucidity of his exposition. But at
this juncture, the Lieutenant of Police, d'Argenson,
took a hand in the game and, on the pressing instances
of unlucky punters, invited Law to leave the country
on the pretext, says a dry contemporary, that he
"knew too much about the various games which he
had introduced into the capital." Law apparently

made no protest, though doubtless he registered a mental note to deal with the importunate Lieutenant of Police on some future and more auspicious occasion. They have long memories in Edinburgh.

After five years spent in scouring Europe, years profitably employed in gambling and speculation, this irrepressible Scotsman heard of the death of Louis XIV and of the appointment as Regent of his crony and admirer, the Duke of Orleans. Swooping down on Paris, he found the country in a truly deplorable situation. The national debt had attained the astronomical figure of three and a half milliards of *livres*, and not only was the treasury empty but the revenues for years to come had been mortgaged at usurious interest. The people, overburdened with taxes, were starving: industry and trade were at a standstill. Despite the harshness of the laws against bankruptcy, liquidation was the order of the day. Thousands of artisans crossed the frontiers and capitalists smuggled their wealth abroad. The depreciated currency attracted hordes of foreigners who battened on the misfortunes of France, whilst at home the detested *traitants*, or tax-farmers, took full advantage of the Government's plight to pile up incredible fortunes.

Law, who realised to the uttermost farthing the hopelessness of the situation and the incompetence of the Council of Finance, came forward with his scheme which was, in brief, the founding of a royal bank operating with paper currency and with the power to act as receiver of all the taxes of France.

" Money," proclaimed the eloquent Law, " is the
blood of the State and must circulate. Credit is to
business what the brain is to the human body."
The proposed bank would establish credit by re-
storing public confidence in the financial competence
of the Government, whilst the use of bank-notes would
stimulate commerce by doing away with the cumber-
some business of transporting specie from one end of
France to the other.

The Government hesitated, though the Regent, who
adored novelties, was enthusiastic. Old hands like
the duc de Noailles and the duc de Saint-Simon
smelt danger in this proposal to establish a State
bank in an absolute monarchy, but Law urged that
no king would be so criminally short-sighted as to
abuse the bank's credit. He generously offered to
forfeit his whole fortune of nearly two millions to
charity if the bank did not in five years restore the
finances of the country. Once the public got accustomed to bank-notes, he urged, they would no longer
want to use specie, especially since the bank was
ready to honour its notes at sight and, moreover,
" *à poids et à titre du jour*," or as we say, at the rate
of exchange of the day of presentation. Meanwhile
the Finance Council, while considering the scheme,
regarded it with suspicion if not with hostility. To
quiet the murmurings of the people it set up the
notorious *Chambre de justice*, nicknamed the *Chambre
ardente*, to investigate the source of the scandalous
fortunes of certain *traitants*. This court, like most in-
struments of repression, flattered at first the righteous

vindictiveness of the populace but speedily became an object of loathing. Some idea of its methods may be gathered from the following decree issued in March 1716:

It shall be legal for anyone who desires to make a denunciation, even for the lackeys and servants of those who come within the jurisdiction of the aforesaid Chamber, to lay their information under their own name or, if they please, *under an assumed name.* . . . We forbid all our subjects, on pain of death, to harm the denunciators by word or deed.

The net results of this inquisition were negligible in proportion to the moral damage inflicted on society. A few notorious financiers like Gruet, Le Normand, and the ex-lackey Poisson, were pilloried and despoiled, but many innocent men fell a prey to the envy of spiteful informers. The general alarm and despondency further paralysed commerce, and soon the Parisians could be heard singing in the streets:

> Cette affreuse Inquisition
> Condamne sans distinction
> Avec le fripon l'honnête homme.
> Devant ces Messieurs c'est tout comme.
> Il suffit qu'on ait de l'argent,
> Ils le prennent impunément.[1]

When in France a public institution becomes matter for the *chansonnier* it is already doomed in the popular mind. Now the clamour arose for a new *Chambre de justice* to try the members of the old one.

[1] This frightful inquisition condemns indifferently the rogue and the honest man, for to these gentlemen they are alike. It is enough for them that you have money which they seize with impunity.

On 2 May 1716 Law got authority to found, not a royal bank but a *banque générale*, a purely private enterprise. At first the new bank excited no great interest: some indeed looked on the Scotsman as rather a simpleton because he accepted, in payment of shares, one-quarter in specie and the remaining three-fourths in the Government bonds or *billets d'état*, then being quoted at eighty per cent below their face value. But when the public discovered that Law's bank-notes could be readily honoured it became rather a smart thing to open a current account at Law's, or *Lass* as the French pronounced it. The bank acquired credit and there was such a general revival in trade that artisans began to return and capital to filter back into France.

Despite the opposition of the Parlement, Law's prestige steadily increased, and in May of 1718 he suggested to the Regent an ingenious though immoral scheme which enabled the Government, by manipulating its State bonds, to clear a profit of fifty per cent. Law was obviously a financier of talent. In August the Parlement, which was apparently too bourgeois to appreciate such gifts, revived an old decree forbidding foreigners under pain of death to meddle with the King's moneys, but the resourceful Orleans swiftly summoned a *lit de justice* and, to the chagrin and great humiliation of the Parlement, annulled its edict and moreover forbade it to interfere in future with affairs of State. By a declaration of 4 December 1718 Law's bank was transformed into a *banque royale*, and orders were issued to the

King's treasurers all over the country to forward taxes to the new centre. The hundred and fifty-three members of the Parlement de Paris, still rankling under the insult inflicted on them on that black Friday of 26 August, had perforce to suffer in silence the fresh ignominy represented by the triumph of the hated foreigner, but these stubborn bourgeois were by no means subdued, as events will show. Noailles, however, had been won round and even the haughty Saint-Simon. D'Argenson was temporarily immobilised by the weight of two magnificent sine-cures, for Law had him appointed Lieutenant of Police and *Garde des Sceaux*, where his activities were restricted to the formality of affixing his seal to the projects engendered by Law and approved by the admiring Regent.

But the establishment of the royal bank was intended by John Law merely as a stepping-stone to a greater enterprise. To keep his promise of honour-ing his notes at par he had, in August 1717, founded the *Compagnie d'Occident* which later became notorious under the title of the *Compagnie des Indes*. Many attempts had been made to float such colonial com-panies in France in the seventeenth century but, partly owing to Dutch and English competition and partly to lack of business acumen, these ventures had not been very successful. When Law arrived on the scene the feeble companies of the East Indies, of China, Senegal, San Domingo, of Canada, and the Barbary States were dying of inanition. Crozat, the milliardaire, had obtained a monopoly of trade in the

Mississippi basin, but even he too had failed. Law took over this privilege and floated the new *Compagnie d'Occident* with sovereign rights in that part of French America which we now call Louisiana and known popularly to Law's contemporaries as "le Mississippi." He had in addition the monopoly of the Canadian fur trade. The original issue of shares amounted to two hundred thousand at five hundred *livres* apiece, but Law was of course hampered by his policy of accepting part payment in the depreciated *billets d'état*. By cornering stocks of furs, however, he kept up prices and soon absorbed the smaller colonial companies which we have mentioned. By May 1719 the *Compagnie d'Occident* had nearly four millions in its coffers and possessed a fleet of twenty ships. The acquisition of the tobacco monopoly in Virginia further raised the price of shares, and the situation looked promising.

But meanwhile the Scotsman had to face serious rivalry in France itself. The rancorous and ambitious d'Argenson, jealous of Law's growing prestige, secretly plotted his ruin. To this purpose he entered into collusion with the four brothers Pâris, typical *traitants*, who had amassed colossal fortunes by speculation and malversation in the closing years of the reign of Louis XIV. The expiration of the lease of certain tax farms called the *fermes générales* gave D'Argenson his opportunity, and by letting these out to his *valet de chambre*, who was of course merely a straw man for the brothers Pâris, the Keeper of the Seals forged a weapon which very nearly proved Law's undoing A powerful rival company thus arose in France itself, with a capital of one hundred millions of *livres*, and, since it accepted depreciated *contrats de rentes* in payment of its thousand-*livres* shares, the prospects of the Mississippi company were by no means bright. The Pâris brothers were, however, handicapped by their reputation as sharks and by the fact that they were not associated with the Government. Their methods had nothing of the Scotsman's artistry, their main object being to milk the taxpayers of two hundred millions during the six years' tenure of their lease.

Law issued new stock, entered on a vigorous campaign of publicity, and did his utmost to encourage speculation in the shares of the company. Every purchaser of the new stock was accorded facilities, and the payment of a premium of fifty *livres* plus twenty-five *livres* deposit ensured delivery of one share. Rumours of the fabulous wealth of the Mississippi were circulated and stories of a rock of emerald in Arkansas, of vast silk factories employing thousands of natives, of fleets laden with ingots of gold were received as gospel by the gullible French public. An old-timer called Cadillac, who had served in Louisiana, was sent to the Bastille for his indelicacy in casting doubts on the veracity of these tales. Law got workmen sent out to America under the engineer Delatour who founded the town we now call New Orleans. The French port of Lorient was also established by the company as an entrepôt for the riches which were expected to pour in from America. The

Compagnie d'Occident, now enlarged by the addition
of the smaller ventures, traded henceforth under the
name of the *Compagnie des Indes* and opened its
offices in the rue Vivienne opposite the *Banque
royale* which was established in the Palais Mazarin
in the wing now occupied by the Prints Department
of the *Bibliothèque nationale*, as Mazarin's palace is
now called.

It was decided that to obtain shares in the new
company one must possess at least four of the old
Occident shares, which were called the *mères* or
"mothers." The new ones were known as the *filles*
or "daughters." The stock rose with incredible
rapidity, and in a month sellers of thousand-*livres*
shares cleared seven hundred per cent profit and still
the price went up. At this stage Law, by tendering
fifty-two as against the forty-eight millions offered
by the Pâris brothers, got their contract annulled
and took over the *fermes générales*, thus disposing of
a dangerous rivalry and making a life enemy of the
furious d'Argenson. Such was the fate of the
"Anti-system."

The famous *système* itself was now, in the summer
of 1719, in the heyday of its prosperity. For eight
hectic months, from June 1719 till February of 1720,
France presented the spectacle of a nation temporarily bereft of its senses. High and low, prince
and lackey, grand duchess and kitchen wench fought
for possession of the magic scraps of paper which
raised their owners overnight from poverty to wealth.
Law, forgetful of the elementary rules of economics,

issued another four million *livres* in notes, but for a time at least he had no fear of a run on his bank for cash: so effective was his propaganda in favour of paper that the public did not want specie. The offices of the company were packed daily with a heterogeneous mob of Parisians, provincials, and foreigners, all eager to buy the coveted shares with which they rushed off to the rue Quincampoix, "the street," as it was known, where the actual broking took place.

The rue Quincampoix still exists and its surroundings have scarcely changed since 1719. Then, as now, it was approached by two streets, the rue Aubry-le-Boucher, the gentlemen's entrance, and the rue des Ours, consecrated to the plebs. Imagine the scene in this narrow malodorous thoroughfare on a broiling July day. Penned in between the chains which are stretched across either end of "la rue" is a screaming, sweating throng in which every rank is represented. The brokers of kings huckster with powerful porters from the markets who by sheer brute force have succeeded in fighting their way into the offices of the company and have run panting from the rue Vivienne to dispose of stock. An enterprising hunchback lends his hump as a desk and makes a fortune of a hundred and fifty thousand *livres* in this strange fashion. The proprietors of houses in the street let their rooms for what they care to ask, and a poor cobbler who for years had plied his craft in a flimsy little shack finds wealth overnight by the simple expedient of fitting it up as an office. The adjacent restaurants are packed with fashionables, some amusedly watching the scene, others issuing orders to their perspiring brokers. Touts dart round the corner to the accommodating Jew usurers who lend money at a quarter per cent per quarter-hour —"clock loans"—and having obtained their bank-notes scurry off to the company, for all shares must be paid for in Law's bank-notes. Frequent fights arise in the rue Quincampoix over this matter as in the case of the *sieur* Cambis who came to blows with a broker who refused to accept specie. Scullions become "carriage folk" and coachmen ride inside their own equipages. One *nouveau riche* absent-mindedly jumps up behind his own coach and to his astonished servant explains angrily that he is just seeing whether the carriage will bear another postilion. All over the country vehicles of every sort are booked up for months ahead, for all France is moving towards "the street." The flower of the aristocracy reap immense harvests in return for their protection. In two years the duc de Bourbon amasses sixty millions and more than a hundred are known to have acquired fortunes of over twenty millions. Crowning irony! John Law's coachman deserts his master. On leaving he says haughtily: "You need a coachman. Choose one of these fellows and I'll take the other." The self-abasement of the nobility is pitiful. Mrs. Law, whom no one believes to be legally married, cannot move without a cohort of purring duchesses, whilst women of the proudest lineage are willing to prostitute themselves for a word

from the Scotsman. Many were the ruses employed
to gain a private audience with Law. One ingenious
lady hired people to shout "Fire!" outside his house,
and when he rushed out approached him for a tip.
Another arranged a carriage accident outside his door,
and it is even said that one lady came down the
chimney of his bedroom. When a party was given
for little Miss Law the papal nuncio led the throng
eager to kiss the child's hand. Contemporaries like
Duhautchamps could scarcely believe their eyes. "It
was like a dream," says that historian; and had he
said "a nightmare" he had been nearer the mark,
for surely never has an aristocracy defiled its honour
to such a degree.

Of Law's connivance in this disgraceful state of
affairs there can be no doubt; but while speculation
was, for the time being, to the advantage of the
company, the avarice of the French people themselves was the sole cause of the excesses which
characterised this period of money madness. To the
financier money as such had no great attraction. His
compelling motive was not the acquisition of a great
personal fortune but the encouragement of commerce,
the establishment of credit, and the financial recu-
peration of France as a result of his "system."
Certain of his acts, indeed, bear the stamp of a
statesmanlike mind. The simplification of taxation
by the abolition of annoying and petty impositions,
the loan of money at two per cent to foster industry,
the relief afforded unfortunate bankrupts, and the res-
titution of moneys illegally extorted by the *Chambre*

de justice must all be written to his credit. But the gambler got the better of the financier, and in his zeal to make a success of the "system" he revealed a complete ignorance of the mind of the people. His appointment as Comptroller-General of Finances, which cost him a mass at Melun, appears to have turned his usually level head. Courted by men who a few months before would have refused him admittance to their table, treated with deference and affection by the Regent himself, received with admiring shouts of "Vivent le Roi et Monseigneur Law," he would indeed have been more than human had he not experienced some stirrings of self-admiration. But soon the tide of popular opinion began to turn. Ribald and satirical songs celebrated his conversion to Roman Catholicism, and many were the allusions to his past career at the gaming-tables and to his fortunate escape from Tyburn tree.

> Law, du gibet fidèle élève,
> Viens-tu te faire pendre en Grève?
> Mais non! Tu viens pour nous régir.
> Tous les échappés de potence
> Sur nos biens ont le droit d'agir.
> On n'en voit point d'autres en France. [1]

As is usual in periods of factitious and scabrous prosperity, the great mass of the people suffered. Prices rose and wages too, but not quickly enough to prevent the inevitable distress which is the lot of the working

---

[1] Law, faithful pupil of the gallows, have you come to get hanged in the Place de la Grève? Of course not! You have come to rule over us. All these escaped gallows-birds have the right to speculate with our property: you don't see any others in France now.

classes on these occasions. Law in encouraging speculation had lighted a blaze which, with all his craft and the resources at his disposal, he was powerless to extinguish. In the train of speculation came a wave of crime and a passion for luxury unparalleled in French history. A particularly brutal murder was committed by the comte de Horn, a young debauchee related to the Regent and to most of the best families in Europe. Horn, aided by two ex-officers, lured a rich Mississippian into a house in the rue de Venise where they did him to death and afterwards disappeared with the sum of a hundred and fifty thousand *livres* which the unfortunate man had just won by speculation. Law took advantage of the opportunity to close the rue Quincampoix. This affair, the culmination of a long series of similar crimes directly arising from the activities of the *agioteurs*, ended in the execution of the comte de Horn who, despite thousands of protests from the aristocracy of Europe, was broken at the wheel on the Place de Grève. "Blood-letting is the only cure for bad blood," said the Regent as he signed the death warrant. There is no doubt that Law's intransigence in this matter influenced Orleans, to whom it was represented that to exercise clemency would be bad for business. Speculation, however, could not be suppressed by the closing of a street, and it continued elsewhere, notably in the Place Vendôme, where tents were erected and side-shows and lotteries set up.

Mention has been made of Law's advertising

methods, and here tragedy and comedy dispute for mastery. To the great joy of the Parisians, who have always had a special weakness for anything savouring of exoticism, the *Compagnie des Indes* imported a dozen samples of the human fauna of the Mississippi region, six young Indian men and six copper-coloured maidens. One of the latter, the Daughter of the Sun, was a queen in her own right, and it occurred to the French Government that it would be a good political move to marry her to a Frenchman. There was, however, one trifling circumstance which was liable to disturb the conjugal bliss. The Daughter of the Sun had the right to order her husband's execution if he failed to give complete satisfaction. Notwithstanding this "saving" clause there were many candidates, and finally a robust and gallant army sergeant named Dubois sailed off to America with his coloured bride. Alas! the reign of Dubois *premier* was a brief one: he displeased the Queen, who was cruel enough to exercise to the full her royal privilege.

Readers of *Manon Lescaut* will recollect the passage describing the brutal deportation of the heroine who, along with a troupe of professionally immoral women, is sent off to America where she is to be married to some rogue, also transported. The author, the good abbé Prévost, was by no means exaggerating, for, in order to populate the newly acquired colony, the *Compagnie des Indes*, with the sanction and the help of the Government, emptied the prisons of young men and women who were marched to La Rochelle, the former on foot and chained, the latter in carts

and sporting yellow ribbons, jeering at the passers-
by; and to the great embarrassment of former clients,
the ladies were wont to shout endearing greetings
from their coign of vantage. The Parisians at first
made up ditties about these blushing brides-to-be.

> Célébrons l'établissement
> De la Compagnie d'Occident,
>   Landerinette,
> Autrement du Mississippi,
>   Landerinette.
>
> Des filles on y enverra,
> Et d'abord on les mariera,
>   Landerinette,
> Si l'on y trouve des maris,
>   Landerinette. . . .[1]

Another song was to the effect that these rogues and
ladies of easy virtue probably represented the most
solid assets of the company, but that was later. Soon
amusement changed to anxiety, for sinister rumours
were abroad as to the fate of these wretches. The
prisoners themselves, terrified by unknown fears,
revolted at La Rochelle and in the prison of Saint-
Martin-des-Champs. But gradually it was realised
how useless these unfortunates were as emigrants and
the company's agents turned their attention to the
poor-houses and orphanages. Now, one of the privileges in the original charter of the company was permission to raise and equip its own troops, called
archers, who, like most irregular units, soon acquired

---

[1] Let us celebrate the establishment of the *Compagnie d'Occident*,
otherwise, the Mississippi. They are sending trulls there, and first
of all they will marry them off, if they find husbands.

an unsavoury reputation for rowdyism, bullying,
and immorality. These ruffians, with their blue and
silver uniforms and their three-cornered hats, swag-
gered about the streets of Paris, and as they
were given a pistole for every arrest, many innocent citizens fell a prey to the rapacity of these
bandouliers du Mississippi. It will probably never
be known to what extent the company abused
its powers, but persistent rumours were current
that more than five thousand young girls over
ten had been abducted. The people, in a frenzy
of panic, gave credence to the wildest tales. It
was said that every third child over ten was to
be seized for transportation. A hundred girls were
supposed to have been thus spirited away from a
very well known conventual foundation, the Hôpital
Sainte-Catherine, which boarded orphan girls free and
found them employment with bourgeois families. A
fracas arose in the Saint-Denis quarter over the arrest
by the *archers* of the son of a rich grocer and the
daughter of a police officer. The mob attacked the
bandouliers, and there were twenty deaths. Parlement insisted that henceforth these brigades of
irregular troops be accompanied by regular police
officials and ordered the lists of deportees to be submitted to it weekly for revision. Despite such danger
signals, Law obstinately adhered to his emigration
scheme, since at all costs the company must be made
to produce immediate results so as to offset the
steadily growing mass of paper being issued by the
bank. But not even the genius of Law could prevent

the inevitable *débâcle*: the famous "system" was cracking ominously and soon new and disquieting developments came to light.

The new year had opened in a dazzling fashion with the Mississippi shares at the amazing figure of eighteen thousand *livres*; in February the *Banque royale* was officially merged with the *Compagnie des Indes*. But Law, with his finger on the pulse of the market, could detect the symptoms of imminent collapse. Holders of his beloved notes began to hanker after cash, and Law, irritated by this illogical behaviour, retorted with the notorious decree of 27 February 1720, which forbade anyone to have in his possession more than five hundred *livres* in gold or silver. Even goldsmiths were prevented from manufacturing articles weighing more than one ounce except, indeed, ecclesiastical crosses. A few days later, too, he arbitrarily fixed the value of shares at nine thousand *livres*. As was to be expected, these measures, far from checking the activity of the *réaliseurs*, intensified it, and soon all the abuses associated with the defunct *Chambre de justice* were revived. Delation again reared its sinister head and the pent-up loathing of the people found an outlet in ugly threats against the person of the hated Scotsman. The toll of mysterious murders increased, for, despite heavy sanctions, the informer took his life in his hands. The High Court judge, Lambert de Vermon, found a way of acquainting the Regent with the feelings of the nation. Approaching him mysteriously, he said: "Monseigneur, I have come to report to you a man who is hoarding fifty thousand *livres* in gold." "Monsieur le président!" exclaimed the Prince, recoiling in disgust. "What sort of —— trade is this you are engaged in!" "I see from your Highness's forcible language," said the judge, "that you share the sentiments of the people in regard to this law you have made. It is myself whom I am denouncing and I hope you will give me the reward offered to informers."

The *arrêt* of 21 May 1720, immediately reducing the value of shares to eight thousand *livres*, with the announcement of a further drop to five thousand, aroused unspeakable indignation and had to be repealed a few days later. Confidence had now completely vanished, and the closing of the bank for the usual quarterly visit of the inspectors created a panic. The Regent was obliged to ask for Law's resignation as Comptroller, but softened the blow by creating him Intendant of Commerce and State Councillor with sword. Now the affrighted dukes and duchesses, terrified at the prospect of losing their swiftly acquired millions, rallied anxiously round the one man who could, with a wave of his magic wand, restore order out of the gathering chaos. But no human agency could stop the run on the bank. The canny Bourbon and the unspeakable Prince de Conti carted away wagon-loads of specie, and when the news went round that the bank would change only one hundred-*livre* note per person there were frightful scenes in the rue Vivienne and in the adjacent rue des Petits Champs, where more than fifteen thousand people

sweated, fought, and cursed in the pitiless heat of
a July day. The gates of the bank courtyard were
opened to admit a few hundreds and then closed by
armed force. Brutish scenes took place. Fifteen
wretches were killed and many maimed by members
of the crowd who clambered on the gates and hurled
themselves on the people beneath. Prices of neces-
sities shot up, for dealers, in spite of threats of prison,
refused to accept the now discredited bank-notes.
Meanwhile the Regent and his roués continued their
nightly orgies at the ill-famed *bals de l'Opéra*. D'Argenson, surprised in an attempt to ruin Law, was
deprived of office and retired to the convent of
Tresnel, the superior of which was his mistress. The
incident prompted some wag to broadcast the following advertisement. "Lost: A big black dog with a
red collar [1] and hanging ears. Finder please communicate with the Abbess of Tresnel and claim reward." His cronies, the brothers Pâris, were exiled
to their estates in Dauphiné. Law then went in
person to the honest d'Aguesseau and persuaded
him to take over the Seals. Under various pretexts
the bank now opened only for short periods and on
certain days when it changed no more than one ten-
livre note per person. Law's carriage was followed
into the Palais Royal by a mob screaming for vengeance. One woman, whose husband had been killed,
hissed in his face: "You ——! If there were only
three other women like me in Paris you would be
torn to pieces." The Scotsman got down and very

[1] A reference to his *cordon rouge*.

deliberately turning on his heel, replied: "Vous êtes des canailles." His coachman, driving off, made a foolish remark about hanging some of these damned Parisians, with the result that in a few minutes the coach was in matchwood and he himself all but mauled to death. Mrs. Law and her daughter now no longer dared show themselves in the streets and the windows of Law's magnificent house in the Place Vendôme were smashed.

It was the bankruptcy of the "system," but Law still played for time. His final effort was to issue an edict whereby the *Compagnie des Indes*, in return for perpetual tenure of its privileges, was to take over six hundred millions of *livres* in notes from the bank. Parlement stubbornly refused to register this decree and the Regent executed a *coup d'état* by exiling all its members to Pontoise on 21 July 1720. The dignified Palais de Justice was given over to roystering dragoons who whiled away the time by holding a mock trial on a dog. In the meantime, speculators like the duc de la Force and the duc d'Antin cornered large stocks of provisions, and the former underwent the humiliation of a public trial. Caricatures of the period represent him as a hawker, staggering under an enormous load of groceries with the legend, "Admirez la Force." But in spite of a rigorous watch kept on the frontier, great sums in specie were smuggled out of the country. Law, like many others, bought up real estate, but solely with the object of showing his continued confidence in the system. And, indeed, had he been dishonest he could quite well have invested these sums abroad. Yet in December, when distress was at its height, Barbier, who was an eyewitness, writes: "Despite the general misery, I have never seen the theatre more brilliant or more crowded than yesterday at the opera." "But," he adds, "even in the best houses there was not a penny to pay the tradesmen, everything being done on credit." On 12 December, Law appeared at the opera where he was regarded with silent and ominous hostility. The bank was now in the hands of a commission of inquiry which was surprised to find the books in perfect order though they revealed a dreadful state of things.

It is difficult to disentangle from the mass of rumours the exact truth as to subsequent events. On the 14th, however, Law went to his estate of Guermande and thence to his marquisate of Effiat in Auvergne. He set out for Brussels on 21 December, stopping, say some, at Paris to arrange certain private affairs with his lawyer. At any rate one thing is certain. Far from taking millions with him, as his enemies alleged, he left France with a few thousand *livres*, the vestiges of a fortune of nearly two millions which he had brought into the country. His wife remained behind and, after settling her private debts, followed him to Holland accompanied by her daughter. William, John's younger brother, was less fortunate and was imprisoned for a short time in the Bastille, from which he was liberated thanks to the protection of the Bourbons. He remained in France where his descendants are to this day.

Once over the frontier, the ruined financier regained something of his gambler's buoyancy and his self-esteem was restored somewhat by the magnificent reception accorded him by the governor who, re-assured by the authenticity of his passports, believed him to be on an important financial mission. Hot on his trail, too, was de Pressy with a request from the Tsar to take over the organisation of the finances of the Russian Empire, a request to which Law regret-fully found himself unable to accede. So great is the prestige which clings to grandeur, even when it takes the form of a bankruptcy of five hundred and twenty-two millions, that October 1721 found John Law on board a British admiral's flagship on his way from Sweden to London where a few days later he was presented to George I. Appropriately enough, the "Lane" put on a special performance of *The Alchemist* with a prologue written for the occasion and highly flattering to the bankrupt. For some years he lived quietly in London and actually corre-sponded with his old friend, the Regent, who disposed of the bankruptcy by the simple method of making a bonfire of all the documents. In 1725, Law, who pined for the old life of continental adventure, was granted a bogus commission to go to Italy, "not for use but for protection," as his creditors were still in full cry. Legend has it that he staked his last thousand pounds on a bet that he could throw double sixes six times in succession—and won! He died obscurely in Venice on 21 March, 1729, and the Parisians, the least vindictive of mortals, dashed off an epitaph which was inserted in the *Mercure de France*.   Here it is:

> Ci-gît cet Écossais célèbre,
> Ce calculateur sans égal
> Qui, par les règles de l'algèbre,
> A mis la France à l'Hôpital.[1]

[1] Here lies that celebrated Scotsman, that peerless mathematician who, by the rules of algebra, sent France to the Poor-house.

ANGLOMANIACS AND FRANCOPHILES

I

In 1685 many thousands of excellent French citizens, adherents of the Protestant faith, were by a stroke of the pen deprived of their religious liberty and virtually exiled. This act of imbecile fanaticism, known to history as the Revocation of the Edict of Nantes, produced repercussions the importance and extent of which can scarcely be estimated. Some three hundred thousand of France's skilled artisans, tradespeople, and professional men moved over the frontiers to Holland, Switzerland, and Germany. It is computed that in addition to these about eighty thousand crossed the Channel, carrying with them valuable industrial processes relating to the manufacture of silkstuffs, hats, and *articles de luxe*. But what was far more serious, these Huguenots wherever they went formed centres of propaganda, veritable arsenals for the manufacture and distribution of ideas hostile to the French Church and State. And this happened at a critical moment in the intellectual evolution of France where, ever since the time of Rabelais and Montaigne, sceptical and anti-religious influences had been gaining ground amongst the *libertins* or freethinkers. It is not surprising, then, to find that among the thousands of Protestant

29

refugees there were large numbers imbued with the new and bold spirit of independent inquiry. Picture, therefore, the feelings of such embittered men suddenly transported from a country where freedom of speech and of the press were unknown, to an England on the verge of revolution, a land where in the very focus of Anglicanism, freemasons, latitudinarians, and nullifidians could write and speak with impunity.

Intoxicated with their new-found liberty, the intellectuals amongst the refugees mastered the foreign idiom and soon a steady stream of translations and adaptations of the great English freethinkers flowed to the printing-presses of Holland and thence, through the wide breaches in the French censorship, into France. The works of Toland, Temple, Collins, Shaftesbury, Woolston, Locke, and a dozen others appeared surreptitiously in Parisian drawing-rooms and in the libraries of quiet country gentlemen. English ideas on literature, philosophy, science, and theology were poured into France to the delight of the *libertins* who found in them the corroboration of views which they had long discussed in centres like the *salon* of Ninon de Lenclos and the notorious *salon du Temple*. By 1719 we find a French newspaper expressing itself in the following terms:

It is sufficient for a book to bear the title "Translated from the English" in order to excite the immediate curiosity of the public. Indeed the majority of Englishmen think and express themselves so happily that one finds in all their works a peculiar characteristic which makes them sought after. Is this a privilege attached to the nation or the result of the liberty which it enjoys? I believe that there is no room for doubt. Freedom of speech and of the press lend to the mind a certain loftiness which lies within the reach of every nation.

Thus the *Nouvelles littéraires*, a representative and influential organ.

The "Rainbow" coffee-house in Fleet Street was the rendezvous of the French colony in London. In this clearing-house of ideas the refugees met with their English and Dutch sympathisers and talked over forthcoming publications. Here might be seen De Moivre the mathematician and Fellow of the Royal Society with his friends Halley and Newton. Boyer, the lexicographer, and founder of the *Postboy*, was the venerable and respected chairman of the group. Motteux, also of the club, started the *Gentleman's Journal* and wrote English plays, while Rapin-Thoyras, another habitué of the "Rainbow," made history with William of Orange at the siege of Limerick before writing it in his celebrated *Histoire d'Angleterre*. Pierre Daudé, who came over as a divinity student, abandoned the Church to devote himself to the dissemination of English philosophic ideas when he was not too busy at the Exchequer where he held a minor post. De Saint-Hyacinthe gave France her first translation of *Robinson Crusoe*. Des Maizeaux, a F.R.S. and a man of European outlook, prepared the first complete edition of Bayle's *Dictionnaire*, the most potent book in France till the appearance of the great *Encyclopédie* of 1751. One might indeed call it the Old Testament of the intelligentsia. A host of journalists lent their pens to this great work of dissemination, and it is literally true that, intellectually speaking, the discovery of England by France was due to the efforts of these exiles. The critic Brunetière, in one of his grandiloquent phrases, speaks of Louis XIV as destroying the moral nerve of his country for the metaphysical satisfaction of hearing Mass chanted in Latin from one end of France to the other. He was contemplating at the moment the loss incurred by Louis of hundreds of high-principled Protestant magistrates and administrators at a time when the French governing classes were sorely in need of such moral ballast to offset the prevailing licentiousness. But, as we have seen, the Revocation of the Edict of Nantes was destined to carry with it consequences of a much more positive and active kind.

In the great days of the reign of Louis XIV it is doubtful whether the whole of France could have mustered a dozen people familiar with the English language and literature. Saint-Evremond of course knew both, but as an exile who resided many years in London he must be looked upon as an exception. The first traveller's account of English manners and customs written in French is to be found in the *Remarks on England* of one G. Lesage who, by the way, was not related to the famous novelist. This Lesage travelled in England in 1710 and 1711, and his observations, though meagre, have a certain interest owing to their novelty. Lesage visited Oxford and Cambridge and found the standard deplorably low. Owing to the inaccessibility of the professors, he was unable to find out anything definite about the prevailing method of instruction, chiefly, we gather, because there was no method at all. He notes, however, that the French system of philosophy as outlined by Duhamel and Leclerc was generally in use, whilst Montaigne's *Essays* were extremely popular.

The English, he observes, are curiously free from jealousy. "In every three Frenchmen one can find two cooks: in every three Englishmen three cuckolds." Towards the south of England there is a tendency to melancholy and here suicide is common—an interesting anticipation of Montesquieu's theory of the influence of climate on character. It is not clear whether Lesage went to Scotland, so that probably the following remarks were acquired from English friends: "The Scots are generally vain and love to talk of their family. They are lazy in their own country but industrious abroad. In England they carry on the trade of mercers as do our Savoyards and Dauphinois in France." Having once sampled the air of England, says Lesage, they rarely return to their own country, and the English, who hate them, say: "If Cain had been Scotch, God would have changed his punishment and condemned him to stay at home." To Lesage Scotland is a wild country inhabited by savages, and by way of illustration he relates the following anecdote. The Duke of Argyll, learning that his tenants were completely ignorant of the Scriptures, proposed sending a missionary to convert them, but was dissuaded by his steward who pointed out that it would be disastrous to teach the

Highlanders that there existed any being greater than the Duke.

There came to London from Holland in 1728 a romantic and chubby ex-Benedictine called Antoine-François Prévost d'Exiles, better known to readers of the immortal *Manon Lescaut* as l'abbé Prévost. About this first visit of Prévost's we know little more than can be gathered from the novel which he wrote when in London, the *Mémoires d'un homme de qualité*, though from a contemporary reference it seems that he obtained a post as tutor in the house of a nobleman. This tutorship he had suddenly to relinquish on account of an affair of the heart. He went hastily back to The Hague infatuated with England and the English.

His novel, which was very popular, contained his impressions of England and the romantic Benedictine was well fitted both by temperament and circumstances to interpret the Anglo-Saxon mind to his compatriots, for in all his writings there is a curiously English streak of melancholy reverie, a tragic, nay melodramatic strain which distinguishes him from other French writers. In his day French novelists were still classic in their indifference to the picturesque details which reveal the differences between nations and individuals, and Prévost was sufficiently a writer of his century to subordinate his description of English manners to the more serious business of portraying the human heart in its traditional struggle with reason and duty. Still, he found time to describe the daily life of the London streets, a visit to Tunbridge Wells, a journey through the south of England. He begs his reader to discard his old prejudices about "perfidious Albion" and to visit this wonderful country where baronets rub shoulders with cobblers and wine merchants, this land of liberty and natural morality.

> There is no country [says Prévost] where you find so much uprightness, so much humanity, such a just conception of honour, of wisdom, and of happiness as amongst the English. The love of the commonweal, the taste for the solid sciences, the horror of slavery and of flattery are virtues which come almost naturally to this happy people: they pass from father to son like an inheritance.

Prévost is obviously the first Anglomaniac. Well informed on English poetry, he admires above all the English theatre for its sublime and tragic force which stirs the most torpid soul. He goes to see *Hamlet*, Dryden's *Don Sebastian*, and Otway's *Venice Preserved* and proclaims the infinite satisfaction he enjoyed. Returning to London in 1733, this time accompanied by a Dutch lady whom he loved but could not marry, he embarked on a series of translations from English writers. Middleton's *Cicero*, Hume's *History of the House of Stuart*, Dryden's *All for Love*, and finally the novels of Richardson, were all rendered into French by this indefatigable man. His own novels reveal his ineradicable fondness for English culture, as the mere titles show: *Le Philosophe anglais*, *L'Histoire de Cleveland, fils naturel de Cromwell*, *Le Doyen de Killerine* (Coleraine).

Meanwhile the Huguenots were disseminating knowledge of English thought and customs in magazines
like the *Bibliothèque anglaise* (1717–28) and the *Bibliothèque britannique* (1733–77). Prévost, not to be
beaten, started the *Le Pour et le Contre*, an encyclopædic
compilation in the taste of the age, in every issue of
which he gave interesting details on English events
in the world of letters, science, fashion, and the arts.
Lovers of Shakespeare may be disappointed at the
reserve shown by Prévost in his praise of *Hamlet*,
Othello, and the *Merry Wives*, but after all he is
more enthusiastic than the majority of his English
contemporaries. The moment was not yet ripe for
a French cult of Shakespeare: it is indeed doubtful
if that nation will ever accord him that admiration
which the Germans have so lavishly showered upon
him. Certainly the eighteenth century, despite the
efforts of Anglomaniacs like Prévost and the two
Shakespearian translators, Le Tourneur and Ducis,
never really understood the genius of the great
Englishman any more than we shall ever savour to
the full the peculiar intellectual charm of Racine.
There are in questions of taste certain gulfs which no
effort of friendship or infatuation can ever bridge.

Voltaire was in London before Prévost and lived
in England from 1727 until 1729, but his famous
Lettres sur les Anglais were not in general circulation
in France until 1734 when they enjoyed the gratuitous
publicity provided by the French Government which
issued a *lettre de cachet* against the author and ordered
the book to be burned by the common hangman.

After such a propitious send-off the *Lettres* could not
fail to be popular, and they were. This visit to
England took place at a critical moment in Voltaire's
intellectual career, for he arrived in London smarting
from the ignominious and cowardly thrashing inflicted
on him by the servants of the duc de Rohan-Chabot.
He would have been more than human, therefore, if
he had not arrived prejudiced in favour of this new
country, where dukes were answerable in law when it
came to breaking even authors' heads. Voltaire, un-
like Prévost, subordinates his English impressions to
a definite plan. In his Letters he reviews the progress
of English thought as revealed in science, philosophy,
and literature. But his underlying motive is everywhere apparent: it is to show by contrast the injustice of the French social system, the fanaticism of
the Church, and to substitute the empiricism of Locke
for the classic rationalism of Descartes. But in
questions of literary taste Voltaire's enthusiasm for
England becomes lukewarm, for here he no longer
felt the need to employ his system of innuendo, convinced as he was that France had nothing to learn
from England in æsthetic matters. On the contrary,
he condemns Shakespeare for having ruined the
English theatre, and his praise of the Englishman's
strength and naturalness is almost nullified by the
ensuing criticism of his lack of taste and of regularity.
The Gravedigger's scene in *Hamlet*, the death of Des-
demona in *Othello*, and the introduction of the common
people into *Julius Cæsar* shocked Voltaire's classic
sense of fitness. Still, he translated the famous

soliloquy from *Hamlet*, but it is clear that he preferred Addison's *Cato*, which at least obeys the "rules." The writers who appeal to him are those who conform to French taste. Pope's *Essay on Man*, for example, is "the most sublime didactic poem in any language," and Congreve is praised because he writes for *la bonne compagnie*.

One wonders whether Voltaire would have cited as great poets men like the Earl of Rochester and Prior, if not to emphasise the honour attaching to the trade of literature in England as opposed to French usage. An earl who is prouder of being a poet than an aristocrat and a potboy who became a plenipotentiary because of his literary genius! Oh! happy country, where artistic merit is rewarded, where an actress like Anne Oldfield is buried in Westminster Abbey, whilst in France an Adrienne Lecouvreur is denied Christian interment because of bigotry.

Prior to his English visit Voltaire had met in France the great statesman and philosopher Bolingbroke, who had married a niece of Mme de Maintenon's. Bolingbroke, who had made France *son autre pays*, spent his time pleasantly in Paris or else at his château de la Source near Orleans. Lionised in the *salons* of Mme de Tencin, of Mme d'Argental, and others, he frequented the notorious Club de l'Entresol, afterwards closed because of the subversive tone of its political conversations. Voltaire who, as a protégé of old Ninon de Lenclos, was also a *libertin*, admired Bolingbroke unreservedly, partly from hero-worship, partly from snobbery.

I found in this illustrious Englishman [he says] all the erudition of his nation and all the politeness of ours. I have never heard our language spoken with more energy and accuracy. This man, who all his life had been immersed in pleasure and in business, has yet found time to learn everything and to remember everything. He knows the history of the old Egyptians as well as that of England. He knows Virgil as well as Milton. He likes English, French, and Italian poetry, but he likes them in different ways because he discerns perfectly their various geniuses.

To young Voltaire the *roturier* here indeed was the ideal, the *homme universel* that Lesage speaks of in *Gil Blas*, and it was certainly memories of his conversations with Bolingbroke which led his steps towards England after the Rohan-Chabot affair.

Close on the heels of Voltaire, the discreet Montesquieu crossed to London from The Hague in 1729 on the Earl of Chesterfield's yacht. His scanty *Notes sur l'Angleterre*, however, in no way reflect the profound influence which this visit was to exercise on the mind of the author of the *Esprit des Lois*. Montesquieu was a political scientist in search of an ideal form of government. Like Voltaire and other intellectuals, he was out of love with the rational and Utopian theories then in the air and a convert to the experimental and realistic philosophy of Locke and his followers. He was in fact on a voyage of observation and arrived in England after an examination of economic and political conditions in Italy, Germany, France, and Holland. This visit marks a capital date in his life.

The liberty of London [he observed] is the liberty of gentlemen: it differs from the liberty of the Dutch, which is that of the *canaille*. . . .   England is at present the freest country in the world, and I make no exception for any republic.   I call it free because the prince has not the power to do any wrong whatsoever, for the reason that his powers are limited by an Act.   Even if a man in England had as many enemies as he has hairs upon his head, nothing would happen to him.

The reserve of the English pleased this aloof aristocrat and jurist.   In answer to an unspoken question he says: "How can the English like foreigners when they do not like themselves?"   And yet Montesquieu the politician regretted the lack of contact between diplomatic England and France, and it struck him as incongruous that the French ambassador in London should live in the isolation created by his ignorance of the foreign tongue and that responsible ministers in Paris should know less about England "than a six-months-old child."

In the meantime France was beginning to raise herself out of the welter of bankruptcy into which she had been cast by the greed of her financiers and nobility and the well-meaning but disastrous speculative schemes of the Scotsman John Law.   The War of the Spanish Succession broke out and did little to increase the popularity of England with the common people and the court politicians, though it made no difference to the steady interchange of ideas.   Intellectual commerce was not interrupted.   Voltaire's *Mort de César*, his "improvement" on *Julius Cæsar*, was produced in 1743: Chesterfield and the fashionable erotic novelist Crébillon the younger exchanged satirical gossip about Richardson's *Pamela* which at first met with indifferent success in France. *Joseph Andrews* appeared in translation in 1744 and was advertised for its picture of English manners though, indeed, the French public was scarcely ready to appreciate the juicy realism of Fielding. A decade was to elapse before the gradual pressure of English literary taste made itself felt in France and until the two races found a definite point of contact in their mutual enthusiasm for the type of literature which appeals to the sentiments rather than to the reason.

An interesting chapter will one day be written about the inroads made in France by Freemasonry, another English importation. We know from the Memoirs of Narbonne, the chief of the Versailles police, that a French lodge existed at the doors of the royal palace. Its Grand Master until 1743 was the duc d'Antin and he was succeeded at his death by the comte de Clermont, a scion of the powerful house of Condé. Several inhabitants of Versailles, many of whom were employed in the palace, became members, but the existence of the lodge was revealed to the police in 1744, owing to the indiscretion of one of the brothers, and this branch was dissolved. But all over France lodges sprang up, and by the middle of the century the Freemasons were established in nearly three hundred French towns with affiliations in the army, in the clergy, and even in the *haute noblesse*.

Just after the war and very possibly during

hostilities, numbers of young Englishmen undertook
the short tour to Paris, Versailles, and Marly.   From
a contemporary guide-book we can form some idea of
the usual procedure adopted by travellers in the reign
of George II.   The trip cost forty-five pounds, in
addition to the expenditure on clothes, for no Englishman could move in French society in a London suit.
Much of this money went into the voracious pockets
of porters and French guides, who "went snacks with
them."   To hire a chaise hung with springs and
"well glassed" cost three guineas from Boulogne to
Paris.   The inevitable halts at Abbeville, Amiens,
and Luzarche, specially noted, by the way, for their
good champagne and "merry landladies," doubtless
made further inroads into the forty-five pounds, but
the hotel expenses in Paris were not outrageous.   The
"Modène" in the rue Jacob, for example, offered an
"apartment up two pair of stairs for a single frugal
gentleman" at a pound a week, which included "bed,
bed-linen, water-bottle, basin, and towels."   Food
sent from the *rôtisserie* cost eight shillings a day,
whilst an excellent *côte rôtie*, "a light, pleasant
drinking wine, and more used to sit over than any
other," could be had for two shillings.   And finally,
when we learn that our young gentleman could dis-
port himself in "a gay and easy chariot" from seven
in the morning till midnight for twelve shillings, we
can but sigh for those good old days that are no
more.

In 1750 that agreeable gossip but wretched dramatist, Mme du Boccage, arrived in London where she

insisted on being presented to George II. In her letters home she complacently narrates her triumphs and unfolds an interesting and intimate picture of London society life. To use a delicate expression, Mme du Boccage was "un peu portée sur la bouche," for she writes lovingly of Lady Montagu's admirable lunches, of the beautiful room with its pretty Chinese furniture, its Pekinese tapestry, and above all the long table with its transparent tablecloth on which repose "a thousand glittering dishes laden with chocolate, biscuits, cream, and a hundred sorts of toast with excellent tea." She loves the English four o'clock dinners with boiled meats, *pudding au gâteau*, and those exquisite chickens with butter sauce! She is enthusiastic on the subject of English ladies, who are as pretty in the house as when walking "like nymphs" in the Mall. She loves their quaint little straw hats, the close-fitting coat, and the little white apron worn by the mistress of the house when she pours out tea. What a pity that in the evening they should spoil it all by imitating the French modes!

Mme du Boccage saw Handel conducting his own sacred concerts, she went to the opera to hear Italian music, and applauded the great Garrick in Shakespeare. What struck her most, however, was the stillness of the English crowds at Vauxhall and Ranelagh. At Lord Chesterfield's she drank the health of Voltaire and Montesquieu, answered questions about the new novelist Marivaux, and chatted with her compatriot Mme le Prince de Beaumont, whose edifying *Misses' Magazine* was in every proper English

porcelain as good as that which we get in France?
He is furious with the abbé Leblanc for stating in
his book that with one or two more virtues the
English would be the finest race in the world. "How
many less vices do they need for that?" sneers
Fougeret.

He rails at the young French "bloods" who, in
imitation of the English *milords*, stride into drawing-
rooms "muffled up in long riding-coats with mud-
bespattered boots, their hair caught up under their
hats with a comb, and a kitchen knife stuck on their
thighs." He agrees with Voltaire as to the genius of
the great English writers, but claims that French
culture prevails in England where the best native
authors are to be found only in the libraries of a
few connoisseurs. Fougeret condemns the ferocity
and licence of the English stage and the Anglomaniac
cabal which would like to raise Shakespeare into the
front rank. Shakespeare, forsooth!—"a madman
who had occasionally a lucid moment."

He impatiently dismisses the much-vaunted English
liberty as the "right to insult the king and to abuse
foreign travellers," and indicates the vexations which
Frenchmen in London are subjected to. Indeed the
only way to escape molestation is to dress in the
English fashion, to copy that brusque, awkward, and
surly manner which accompanies all their actions, to
twist a man's wrist in token of friendship, to be
impolitely civil, to affect negligence so far as to
appear at the play in curl-papers, and to display in
general the table manners of a pig. "But," concludes

Fougeret, "there are some good points about England. They have fine horses, excellent dogs, and no monks or wolves."

II

War in the eighteenth century was not carried out with that "thoroughness" which is the pride of our modern militarists. Otherwise we should have to regard the period from 1756 to 1763 as a zone of silence in the field of social and literary interaction. Happily this was not the case. Then, as now, spy scares and stories of the inhuman treatment of prisoners by the English were invented by idle politicians for the delectation of the ignorant and sensation-hunting public. But foreign travellers, including English nationals, moved about freely, provided their papers were in order and an English *chargé d'affaires* remained in Paris, though subjected to discreet police supervision. And during the Seven Years War between 1776 and 1783 there appeared the first complete translation of Shakespeare into French, done by a certain Le Tourneur. This, following on La Place's eight-volume *Théâtre anglais*, found the French public in a peculiarly receptive frame of mind, for in 1751 Garrick had visited Paris, leaving a profound imprint on the minds of auditors like Collé the playwright who, although a staunch traditionalist, confessed that Garrick's rendering of the dagger scene from *Macbeth* filled his audience with terror. Already, in 1748, the translation of Lillo's *London Merchant* had drawn tears from the eyes of sentimental Parisiennes, who had a few years before been accustomed to weep deliciously at the "whining" comedies of the Frenchman, La Chaussée. That the public could now tolerate comedies at which one not only laughed, but cried, was but the first step along the road which was to lead through the sentimentalism of Rousseau to the Romanticism of the nineteenth century. Meanwhile opinion was sharply divided as to the merits of Shakespeare and Richardson, though the latter's *Clarissa Harlowe*, as toned down by Prévost, had more admirers than critics.

A contemporary French journalist, discussing the vogue for English literature and customs, claimed that the movement could be attributed to the predominant influence of women in French society of the eighteenth century. To a great extent, of course, he was exaggerating, but thousands of sentimental women on both sides of the Channel found in the novels of Richardson, Rousseau, and imitators like Baculard d'Arnaud, an echo of their intimate yearnings. Diderot, in a fiery and declamatory eulogy, could hardly find adequate language to proclaim the greatness of Samuel Richardson. It became the fashion in France to read only *romans anglais*, or at least French adaptations or imitations of English novels, though most frequently the only Anglo-Saxon characteristic of such fictions was the impossible virtue of their heroines and their English-sounding titles. The focus of French Anglomania now slowly shifted from the England of science and philosophy to the

England of sensibility. Already announced in the novels of Prévost, the Englishman as conceived by the French public, the "stage Englishman," gradually assumed the form of a cross between a Sir Charles Grandison and a Hamlet, impossibly altruistic, ludicrously sentimental, and above all, gloomily eager to shuffle off this mortal coil at the slightest provocation. The graveyard poetry of Young and Hervey and the translations of Macpherson's *Ossian* met with incredible success, and swiftly there arose in France a school of poets and novelists devoted to the cult of this new, sombre genre.

The close of the war, in 1763, was celebrated in France by the production of Favart's peace play, *L'Anglais à Bordeaux*, and the same year saw a great coming and going of celebrities, both French and English. Horace Walpole, indeed, estimates the number of English visitors who passed through Calais from 1763 to 1765 at forty thousand, and a current number of the *Scots Magazine* corroborates this figure. George Selwyn, back from Paris, told Walpole that the English passion for everything French was nothing to theirs for everything English. Parisian hostesses, like the old Maréchale de Villars, anxious to make their English guests feel at home, made Selwyn smile at their ignorance of English customs. Thus the Maréchale, in the middle of a "vast dinner" in honour of the Duchess of Bedford, suddenly exclaimed in tragic accents: "Oh! Jesus! They have forgot! Yet I bespoke them, and I am sure they are ready. You English love hot rolls!" And the guests had per-

force to do justice to an enormous dish of hot rolls
swimming in melted butter. Young men about town
in Paris adopted English dress and sports. It became
the fashionable thing to take boxing lessons, to have
fights with porters in the *Halles*, the French Covent
Garden, or to drink in the company of cabmen.
Horse-racing and betting became all the rage, and
a *Newmarket français* was opened in 1775 in the
Sablons plain with a little belvedere in the middle
for the Queen, who used to order the little English
jockeys to be presented to her. The comte d'Artois,
the duc de Chartres, and other enthusiasts entered
horses, the former sending to England for two animals
which cost him forty-two thousand francs apiece.
Young Guards officers squandered fortunes, and when
horse-racing was forbidden, raced on foot or in cabrio-
lets. That famous Anglomaniac Lauraguais, just
home from London, was asked by Louis XV what he
had learned there. "To think, Sire," was the reply.
"Of horses, you mean," retorted the King, who
considered that these English innovations were
ruining his kingdom.

A letter written in 1769 by Lauraguais to an
English lady pictures the changes that had come
over Parisian society:

We are all metamorphosed into English. A strange and
sudden revolution has happened in our dress, equipages,
furniture, kitchens, and diversions. Our *petits-maîtres*, who
formerly were dressed, perfumed, and painted like dolls at
ten o'clock before noon, ride after breakfast in the Cours la
Reine, the Champs Élysées, and all the environs of Paris in a

plain shirt and frock like your jockeys. Our delicate ladies who never ventured to stir out in the morning run all over Paris and in the public walks in the genteel and loose dress of milkmaids. Our carriages are neat, plain, and convenient. Horse-races are frequent in the Île de France: our stables are full of English hunters and grooms, and our whips, saddles, and boots manufactured by your countrymen who have reduced ours to beggary. We have substituted paper for the tapestries of the Gobelins and introduced in our kitchens roast beef and pudding in lieu of our soups, ragouts, and fricassees. We hunt, swear, and drink toasts and determine all disputes by wagers, like your nobility and gentry. Our girls, who were never allowed to pay or receive visits without a mother or aunt and were shut up in a nunnery till they were often forced to marry a man whom they detested to acquire the privilege of having an intrigue with a fop of their own choice, resort to all places of diversion without control or restraint. Our prostitutes are raised by old debauchees to the rank of countesses and return the disdain of the court to the citizens. Our new Vauxhall is the rendezvous of the most celebrated beauties and courtesans and the prelude to the *petits soupers* and revels of the night. Six millions have already been subscribed towards building a Ranelagh House. In fine, we want nothing but the immense fortunes of your gambling lords and arrogant nabobs to equal them in profusion and debauchery.

Whist, another importation from across the Channel, swept the *salons*.

> Whisk aimable, whisk séduisant,
> Tu charmes ma bergère;
> Il faut que tu sois amusant,
> On te joue à Cythère—

and at Cytherea or Fontainebleau, an ex-Indian

colonel named Smith, who was on the most insolently familiar terms with the royal family, won a fortune of a million and a half francs from the young princes. Walpole, commenting on the craze for whist, says: "They constantly tip a rubber before supper, get up in the middle of the game, finish it after a meal of three courses and dessert, and add another rubber to it."

French visitors to London like Mme de Boufflers, Lauraguais, Lalande, and others brought back wonderful descriptions of Vauxhall and Ranelagh. Lalande, the astronomer, was particularly delighted with the latter resort, and notes in his Diary:

I was surprised at the spectacle. More than a thousand people. One takes tea, coffee, butter, etc. Waiters are numbered; the music, instrumental and vocal, every quarter of an hour. The fireplace resembles an altar surrounded by benches and tables. Spirit lamps on tables. Women hatless and men without swords. The music ends at ten, but there are people till after midnight. . . . Gardens illuminated, delightful by moonlight.

So, in 1770, after a great deal of petitioning, the Parisians had what Walpole sarcastically refers to as their "chalk and pasteboard Ranelagh" in the Champs Élysées. This place, built at a cost of two millions, was never popular despite attractions like cockfighting, *fêtes pyrrhiques, hydrauliques et étrangères.* The Paris Vauxhalls were much more frequented, particularly that of Torré, which opened in 1768 as a sort of fair, but its name was changed to Vauxhall in the following year. The Ruggieri brothers gave wonderful pyrotechnic displays and there were *cocagnes*, concerts, lotteries, and women. However, as this place was only good for fine weather, a winter Vauxhall was opened in imitation of the one in Oxford Street. Le Noir, the architect, produced a fine edifice, a miniature fairy palace in blue and gold. It drew large crowds of English and Parisians because it was the only place where it was correct for women to dance in public and, moreover, went on after the theatres were closed. There was still another Vauxhall on the Boulevards, but it was never a success.

A curious feature of the French *engouement* for things Anglo-Saxon was the extraordinary vogue for English gardens which is intimately connected with the "back to nature" movement reflected in the literature of the time. The so-called "English gardens" seem to have been originally due to an English craze for Chinese horticultural art, which favoured stunted trees, miniature bridges, streams and ponds with winding alleys breaking the perspective and producing the illusion of picturesque disorder. The famous gardens of Kew were much admired by French visitors, and soon all over France those who could afford it installed imitations with tiny pagodas, artificial ruins, grottos, labyrinths, romantic glades, and aviaries of exotic birds. Walpole, who was annoyed because Mme de Boufflers did not admire his neo-Gothic house at Strawberry Hill, ridiculed the fashion for gardens *à l'anglaise*. Describing a famous example belonging to M. Boutin, he says:

M. Boutin has tacked a piece of what he calls an English garden to a set of stone terraces with steps of turf. There are three or four very high hills almost as high and exactly in the shape of a tansy pudding. You squeeze between these and a river that is conducted by obtuse angles into a stone channel and supplied by a pump, and when walnuts come in I suppose it will be navigable. There is a strip of grass, another of corn, and a third *en friche* exactly in the order of beds in a nursery.

A Mrs. Cradock in her Journal describes one she saw in Toulouse at the close of the century:

It is a piece of ground irregularly shaped and quite flat. You see an artificial mountain with a cascade painted on wood. At the top of the mountain a little windmill out of which emerges a figure of a woman looking at a miller who is arriving with a donkey laden with sacks. At the bottom of the mill there is on one side a cottage with open door revealing a spinning-wheel; on the roof a dovecot with pigeons. On the left, outside and quite near the cottage, an old man, a young man, and a dog and pig. The young man is offering grass to three sheep which are feeding at his feet; a cow is lying a little farther off. All these figures, painted to represent life, are absolutely ridiculous.

The duc de Chartres spent a million francs on this amusement, whilst the Queen altered the gardens of the Trianon, including the famous botanical garden of Louis XV, and installed English gardens. Travellers in England like Contant d'Orville were struck with the absence of that classic simplicity in garden designing as immortalised by Le Nôtre in the seventeenth century. Monstrous yews shaped like animals and birds everywhere met his eye, and he chuckles over a catalogue[1] advertising a group of yews clipped to resemble the Garden of Eden. "Adam slightly damaged by the fall of the tree of knowledge in a storm. Eve and the serpent in good condition."

The devotees of the sombre literature *à la* Young found an exquisite pleasure in solitary meditations amongst the crumbling ruins and winding, shady paths of these gardens, which, says Caraccioli, were fine for misanthropes but little use for sociable people. These were the enthusiasts who objected to the French version of Otway's *Venice Preserved* because it left out the tolling of the funeral bell, the scaffold, and the executioners. Alas! In a few years even the most morbid were to have their fill of such violent sensations.

An *Epistle* on English gardens appeared in which the author satirised:

> Ce pont soutenu par de frêles machines,
> Tout ce grotesque amas de modernes ruines,
> Simulacres hideux dont votre art s'applaudit,
> Qu'est-ce? qu'un monstre infirme, un enfant décrépit.

It is only fair to Jean-Jacques Rousseau to say that, though he was the high priest of the new movement towards nature, he was not in sympathy with such excesses. The English garden which he describes in his *Nouvelle Héloïse* reflects his love of wild, untamed nature, and is the antithesis of the grotesque artificialities beloved by his more irresponsible admirers. But external nature having been pitchforked out of French literature, came back with a rush, and soon Marie Antoinette, with her ladies attired in the

[1] This is the burlesque catalogue in the *Guardian*, written by Pope.

smartest "pastoral" modes from Rose Bertin's shop, was successfully managing a model dairy farm at the Hermitage in the grounds of the Trianon. A rustic craze in millinery arose and hats were trimmed with every sort of flower and vegetable, even to dandelions and carrots. One enterprising lady, the widow of an English admiral, had a hat trimmed with gauze to represent a stormy sea with tiny ships—a touching compliment to the memory of her deceased husband. High poke bonnets came into fashion, and when conservative grandmothers frowned these *bonnets à la bonne maman* could be conveniently lowered by pulling a string. Sentimentality found an expression in the names given to these creations—"stifled sighs" and "bitter complaints" being much in vogue.

Most of the Englishmen of note in the fields of literature, science, and politics visited France in the second half of the eighteenth century. Chesterfield, Garrick, Hume, Walpole, Sterne, Gibbon, Adam Smith were well-known personalities in French society, whilst England extended an equally cordial welcome to notables like Helvétius, d'Holbach, La Condamine, Lalande, Beaumarchais, and Grimm. Voltaire gradually lost his early enthusiasm for England, chiefly because of the rising vogue for Shakespeare which annoyed him intensely. However, he never abandoned his admiration for English philosophy, and to the end Locke and Newton remained his idols. "The innkeeper of Europe," as he called himself, he continued to receive large numbers of English admirers at Ferney. But, as he said wryly, they were "so

much in love with their own country that not one
remembered me after his departure." Whilst the
sage of Ferney was, like Candide, "cultivating his
garden" and, in general, leading the life of an English
squire, his old friend Mme du Deffand kept open
house in her apartment in the convent of St. Joseph
for the intellectuals of all nations.   Here in particular
she received Horace Walpole, the satirical, brilliant,
and snobbish cosmopolitan whose letters are a mine
of information on the London and Parisian society
of his time.   In the course of his long life Walpole
visited France six times.   He was a familiar figure
in the *salon* of Mme Geoffrin, the wife of a glass
manufacturer and "the most rational woman in the
world."   In this *salon*, which, says Sainte-Beuve,
was one of the institutions of the century, he met
artists like Van Loo, Vernet, Boucher, though as a
rule Monday was reserved for painters and Wednes-
day for men of letters.   But Walpole, who had written
five volumes on the history of English art, qualified for admission to both assemblies.   Chesterfield,
writing to Stanhope, refers to this remarkable woman
as "most witty in company"; but it was not so much
her wit as her hard common sense and her capacity as
a good listener and generous hostess which attracted to
her *salon* in the rue Saint-Honoré men like Marivaux,
Voltaire, Montesquieu, Lord Albemarle, the British
ambassador, the malicious abbé Galiani, Caraccioli,
the witty Neapolitan representative, the Count de
Creutz, the Swedish minister, Marmontel the novelist
and admirer of Richardson, d'Alembert the encyclo-

pædist—in a word, the flower of Europe's intellectual
aristocracy.

Walpole, who disliked the advanced views of the
philosophes, gradually deserted Mme Geoffrin for Mme
du Deffand, with whom, in 1765, he entered into an
intimate relationship that gave rise to a famous
correspondence. In part owing to Walpole's influence, and partly to the defection of her companion,
Mlle de Lespinasse, who was followed by many of
the *philosophes*, Mme du Deffand lost her excessive
admiration for their doctrines, though she kept up a
prolonged correspondence with Voltaire. One of the
most pathetic episodes in the history of letters is the
romantic passion of this blind septuagenarian for
Walpole, who was over twenty years her junior. The
latter used to rebuke his old friend in the harshest
language, terrified lest the old lady's sentimental
indiscretions should compromise him in the eyes of
a society which was prepared to condone any moral
lapse but not the enormity of making oneself ridiculous. So poor Mme du Deffand, summoning up the
resources of her reason and former scepticism, succeeded in persuading herself that her love was but
maternal affection, an arrangement which Walpole
grandly accepted. For, apart from his petty amour-
propre, he had no desire to break what was possibly
the one sincere friendship of his life.

We have noticed that by the second half of the
century the French intellectuals had far outstripped
their English colleagues in the audacity of their
opinions, particularly in their attitude towards religion

and morality.   One can see the growing rift reflected
in Walpole's growing irritation.   "The savants, I
beg their pardon, the *philosophes*, are insupportable,
superficial, overbearing, and fanatic.   They preach
incessantly, and their avowed doctrine is atheism;
you would not believe how openly—don't wonder if
I should return a Jesuit.   Voltaire himself does not
satisfy them. One of their lady devotees said of him:
'Il est bigot, c'est un déiste.'"   Walpole was out of
humour with compatriots like the Earl of Findlater
who had come over "to suck wisdom from this curious
school of philosophy," and was deeply shocked, when
at dinner with d'Holbach, to hear atheism discussed
in the presence of the servants.   He therefore cultivated more and more the company of "people of
quality," who did not hold materialistic views, and
when at Twickenham, Mme Necker, thinking to please
him, called him a *philosophe*, he was furious at being
compared to a "being compounded of d'Urfé and
Diogenes, a pastoral coxcomb, and a supercilious
brute."

Garrick arrived on his second visit to France in
September 1763, and remained for two years on the
Continent, where he enjoyed an ovation unique in
the annals of the stage of any country.   There is no
doubt but that his reputation helped to improve the
social status of his French colleagues, who were still
outlawed by the Church and oppressed in other ways.
Garrick's first act was to have a medal struck by
Gravelot in honour of the famous actress Mlle Clairon,
to the secret and malicious amusement of Parisian

society which could not, or would not, disassociate Clairon the tragic actress and Clairon the *grande amoureuse*. Garrick's drawing-room performances made a deep impression, and his great admirer, Suard, found that the translations which he had issued to the audience were superfluous, so vividly did the great London actor communicate his meaning by gesture and by accent. It was Garrick's dream to have a constant interchange of English and French troupes, but unhappily this was never successfully effected till after the Revolution.

Vying with Garrick in the public favour, Hume carried the *salons* by storm and, says Charlemont, his "broad unmeaning visage" could be seen at the play amongst the pretty faces of society darlings who scrambled to get beside him. Mme Geoffrin greeted him affectionately as "mon gros drôle," and he writes complacently of his reception by Mme de Pompadour and of meeting the sons of the Dauphin, who were brought specially to pay their compliments in English to the historian. Walpole was chagrined to learn of Hume's brilliant success, and in a letter sarcastically refers to the Scotsman "who very gratefully admires the tone of Paris, having never known any other tone." Unintentionally, I am sure, it was Walpole who embroiled Hume with Rousseau in the famous affair of the bogus letter. Walpole, whose sense of humour was, like his artistic taste, somewhat Gothic, circulated a letter purporting to be from Frederick of Prussia to Jean-Jacques in which the latter was ridiculed and accused of ingratitude. Shortly before

this, Hume, out of the kindness of his heart, had
arranged with a Mr. Davenport to accommodate
Rousseau and his servant-mistress Thérèse Levasseur
in a country house at Wootton. Rousseau, who was
at the time suffering from persecution mania, after
having suddenly decamped from Wootton, wrote to
Hume an amazing letter saying that his horrible
designs were known. Rousseau was later persuaded
that Hume had had no share in the authorship of
the bogus letter, but his disordered mind associated
Hume, the *philosophes*, and Walpole as involved in a
gigantic network of conspiracy contrived to enmesh
him. He referred to a "terrible look" which he had
once surprised on Hume's face and accused him of
having muttered in his sleep the sinister words, "Je
tiens Jean-Jacques Rousseau!" Eventually Hume
found it necessary to refute these charges publicly,
and the absurd affair became a European event. The
upshot was that the *philosophes*, whom Walpole
despised, applauded his trick, whilst Rousseau's
friends very rightly judged it to be the act of a
buffoon. Hume came out with flying colours, to the
chagrin of Walpole who was annoyed at the publicity
given to the affair.

Although Sterne's *Tristram Shandy* had not yet
appeared in its French garb it was known to the
élite through the *Journal encyclopédique*, so that its
author when he arrived in Paris was an object of
sympathetic curiosity. Before going the rounds of
the *salons*, which he did in 1762, Sterne enjoyed himself "shandying," as he called it, in the English

colony in the Faubourg Saint-Germain and through
Garrick obtained his entrée into the society of Mlle
Clairon and of Préville whose low-comedy acting he
much admired. But, curiously enough, his time was
largely spent in the company of the atheistic d'Holbach and his brother *philosophes*. It is difficult at
first to see what particular pleasure the sentimental
Laurence could have found in the camp of these
enemies of Rousseau, but the *philosophes* were also
to some extent *âmes sensibles*, though their sensibility
was not of the declamatory kind. With these "citizens of the world" sentiment found an outlet in the
cult of friendship, humanity, and philanthropy. In
Diderot, however, Sterne found a kindred spirit.
Both were garrulous, emotional, and fervent admirers
of the experimental philosophy of Locke which had
supplanted Cartesian rationalism in France at the
turn of the century. There is also more than a
suspicion that Diderot had remembered *Tristram
Shandy* when he wrote *Jacques le Fataliste*, though
it would be wrong to say, like Professor Cross, that
Diderot "paraphrased and imitated" the Englishman's famous novel. He parodied it.

Sterne, who had a chameleon's gift of adaptability,
soon outdid his hosts in politeness and won the
friendship of such very different people as Mme
Geoffrin, the comte de Bissy, the duc de Choiseul,
the financier Riche de la Popelinière, and above all,
Suard, that great lover of the English who found in
Sterne a fascinating subject for observation. The
"chevalier Shandy," as Choiseul called him, spent

six happy months philosophising, taking notes, and giving free rein to his emotions. One day, for example, found him weeping with his barber over the victims of a fire at the fair of Saint-Germain: the next he was seized by the sudden impulse to kneel in front of the statue of Henri IV, shouting to a delighted crowd to come and imitate him. No wonder that Paris society missed him when he finally left, in June, to recover his shattered health in Toulouse. In this town which, like so many other French provincial capitals, had now its annual quota of English tourists, he met Smollett, a valetudinarian too, but of a different sort. The irascible author of *Peregrine Pickle* was no Francophile. His *Travels* teem with expressions of his disgust for everything French— their vanity, insincerity, curiosity, the uncleanliness of their personal habits, and above all the discomfort of their inns and the insolence of their innkeepers.

In 1763 a number of distinguished French scientists crossed over to England. Louis Dutens, philologist and antiquary, liked the country so much that he remained as chaplain to Stuart Mackenzie. Lalande, the famous astronomer, had come over on behalf of the *Académie des Sciences* to receive communication of the details regarding Harrison's chronometer. Lalande attended the meetings of the Royal Society and the dinners at the "Mitre" club founded by Halley. Here he met his compatriots, Duclos, La Condamine, Camus, and Berthoud, all members of the Royal Society. Duclos, later secretary of the French Academy, was in London for a brief and enjoyable

period of exile owing to some injudicious remarks
which he dropped concerning a duel between the duc
d'Aiguillon and his friend M. de la Chalotais. De la
Condamine, one of the most eccentric men of his age,
was a source of delight to the London street urchins,
for he was deaf and invariably went out armed with
an ear trumpet, a large map, and an umbrella, then
a novel sight. Whilst in London he infuriated his
landlady by the noise he made shouting to his servants, and she asked him to leave. The scientist
refused, so she dressed up two men as constables with
a bogus order for eviction. La Condamine there-
upon wrote to the press declaiming against the
barbarity of the English, and the affair created much
excitement. The popular duc de Nivernais, too, had
just arrived to negotiate the peace treaty. A lover
of the arts and a very gallant soldier and astute
diplomat, it was he whom Chesterfield held up as the
model of the *gentilhomme accompli*. Through him
men like Camus, the mathematician, La Rochette,
the agricultural expert, Lescallier, the naval authority
and orientalist, Lapeyre, the distinguished surgeon,
were ushered into the society of English men of
science. The celebrated chevalier d'Éon, who was
minister plenipotentiary under Nivernais and a great
favourite of George III, was also in London in 1763,
as was Mme de Boufflers, the well-known Anglomaniac. The French visitors were intensely interested
in English domestic politics, and it was fashionable
to visit the notorious Wilkes who, when he went to
Paris in 1768, found all the society women carrying

mouchoirs à la Wilkes with his portrait printed on one side and on the other his famous letter to the inhabitants of Middlesex.

"Towards 1750," says Voltaire, "the nation, sated with poetry, tragedies, comedies, and operas, with romances, romantic histories, with moral reflections more romantic still, and theological disputes on grace and agriculture, began to argue about wheat." In this well-known passage he was referring to the origins of the first French school of political economists, later celebrated under the title of *physiocrates*, whose doctrine was briefly that the prosperity of France depended not on commerce but on agriculture. Vincent de Gournay, the pioneer of the movement, was familiar with such English works as King's *British Merchant*, Child's *Interest on Money*, and Gee's *Causes of Decline of Commerce*, and he disseminated the ideas he found in such works. Turgot, in 1753, arranged for a translation of Tucker's *Essay on the Present State of English Commerce*, and the newly founded *Journal économique*, from 1752 onwards, regularly printed extracts from English economic publications. Montesquieu's son, Secondat, translated Gee's *Considerations on Trade and Navigation*, whilst the ideas of men like Culpepper, Petty, and Davenant were eagerly examined by French thinkers. Mirabeau, the author of the popular *Ami des Hommes*, gleaned his first lessons on economics from the *Essai sur la Nature du Commerce en général* by Cantillon, an Irish banker long resident in France, who died mysteriously in London in 1734. Hume's

essays on politics and commerce were translated, and
during his stay in France he became a close friend of
Turgot, whom he met at the house of d'Holbach.
It was also at the house of this materialist and *philosophe* that Adam Smith discussed political economy
with Turgot, who after his retirement kept up a
correspondence with the author of the *Wealth of
Nations*. Adam Smith, who was travelling tutor to
the young Duke of Buccleuch, made the acquaintance
at Versailles of Quesnay, the King's physician and
chief of the *physiocrates*, or, as they were popularly
known, the "*laissez faire* and *laissez passer*" school
of economists. Morellet, with whom Smith also had
conversations, was probably more intimate with
English economic conditions than any of his colleagues, and in the course of a visit to England made
a point of seeing Tucker and other economists. He
also visited Birmingham, York, Bristol, and other
industrial and trading centres. In 1765, the *Scots
Magazine* voiced the fear that the French were on
the point of outstripping Great Britain in agriculture,
since royal premiums had been offered to encourage
farming and thirty-two societies founded for the same
purpose. There were signs, too, of an increased interest in the future of industry, and as early as
1760 Holker advocated the introduction of English
machinery into France, and another Englishman,
Milne, used English looms in his factory at La
Muette. However, it was not until well into the
eighties that Arkwright's and Cartwright's looms
were employed to any extent in France, when, thanks

to the initiative of men like the duc d'Orléans, the manufacture of cotton goods was begun on a fairly big scale at Montargis, Orleans, and other centres. The "jennys" increased greatly in number by 1789, but it was not till the nineteenth century that any great development took place in France. English methods were also introduced into the French smelting industry, and the great firm of Le Creusot adopted our machines as did also the foundry of Indret, though, as M. Sée points out, these must be looked upon as exceptions and can only be regarded as symptoms of the real industrial revolution which came fifty years later.

The American War of Independence did not essentially interrupt the influx of English ideas, since *américomanie* was but another aspect of Anglomania, and, political views excepted, there was nothing to differentiate Franklin, the popular Paris idol, from a dozen other English thinkers of his day. There was no lack of critics to deplore what many thought was the anglicising of France, although, significantly enough, their strictures bear mostly on the superficial evidences of English imitation—costume, sports, gardens, and other forms of *snobisme*.

> Courons aux drames ténébreux,
> Qui nous tournent la tête:
> Faisons des paris ruineux
> En l'honneur d'une bête.
> Formons un nouveau Newmarket,
> Que le spleen nous dévore.
> Fumons, jouons au cabaret,
> Le jockey vit encore.

These sarcastic lines in Marchand's *Fruits de l'Automne* (1781) are typical of the anti-English criticism of conservative Frenchmen. Others, like Rigoley de Juvigny, confused Anglomania with *philosophisme*, though, as we have seen, the *philosophes* had already gone far beyond the limits reached by their English colleagues. It is of course difficult to judge how deeply English influence penetrated the strata composing French society. John Moore, a cautious observer, notes in the seventies, whilst on a visit to France, that "the philosophical idea that kings have been appointed for public conveniency; that they are accountable to their subjects for maladministration or for continued acts of injustice and oppression, is a doctrine *very opposed to the general prejudice of this nation*." He insists that admiration of the British Constitution is confined to the intellectuals. The bourgeoisie, when told of the limited powers of the English Crown and aristocracy, said pityingly: "C'est peu de chose d'être noble chez vous." Instinctively they would have subscribed to the truth underlying the vinous quip thrown out by the Bishop of Londonderry just before the Revolution, when there was much talk in the air of adopting the British Constitution: "How can you expect a nation which can drink sparkling wine at its meals to get along with the constitution of a people whose only drink is thick, heavy porter?" The taciturnity of the English, as we have seen, gave rise early in the century to the impression fostered by travellers like Prévost that this silence concealed a profound erudition and reflectiveness. They might have remembered the ox in La Fontaine's fable which was silent because it had nothing to say, but instead the legend of the silent thoughtful Englishman gained ground in eighteenth-century France. People began to study the English language, and in 1764, says the *Scots Magazine*, "there were four well-frequented academies in Paris for the teaching of the rudiments of the English tongue." The ability to converse in English became "an indispensable accomplishment for persons of any degree of breeding," and conversation clubs were formed like that in the Hôtel d'York where French was forbidden. Caraccioli complained that he could not move in Paris without stumbling over people reading—servants and masters, at the doors of houses, in carriages, and on the Pont-Neuf, were all to be seen book in hand. "This fury for reading," he was told, came from across the Channel, and he claims that the French have lost their individuality and charm and have become serious and absent-minded like the English.

On the other hand, English observers like Andrews and Walpole could point to many examples of the infiltration of French customs into England. Here again one must guard against travellers' exaggerations. Some few society women set up *salons* in imitation of those in Paris; ladies of the smart set began to adopt cosmetics; England had her *femmes savantes*, and conversation, like books, was freely interlarded with French idioms; English lads, just back from school in France, alarmed their parents with their "Parisian gallantry"; at the outbreak of the Revolution some of the "Bucks, Bloods, and Fellows of Fire" had themselves ejected from London clubs for their indiscreet praise of Jacobinism. On the whole, however, Francophiles were not so common in England as Anglomaniacs in France. English visitors to France outnumbered French travellers in England by twenty to one because, owing to the greater prosperity of our country, foreign travel was within the reach of the middle classes, and this was not the case in France. But to a reader of the memoirs and journals of the time it is clear that whilst the English aristocracy mingled with the French nobility, the rank and file, as to-day, herded together in little clubs and coteries, "keeping themselves to themselves," as they would say, and opposing to French hospitality and curiosity a characteristically English spirit of reserve, of criticism, and of unshakable belief in the superiority of Anglo-Saxon solidity over the frivolity and suspicious vivacity of the French.

L'ABBÉ COYER—A SOCIETY IN TRANSITION

WITH the comfortable perspective of more than one hundred and fifty years it is now almost possible to generalise on the literature of eighteenth-century France. Here is a nation which was too socially self-conscious to produce a work even remotely comparable in artistic beauty to a Racinian play or a poem by Alfred de Vigny. For the literature of the age of Voltaire, Diderot, and Jean-Jacques Rousseau is essentially a literature of ideas, that is to say, a literature of propaganda. It was so to such a degree that it is wellnigh impossible to point to a single novel or even a poem which was not written with a definite social purpose. The tragedies of Voltaire, the dramas of Diderot, the writings of Rousseau and Montesquieu, the novels of Marivaux, Prévost, and Crébillon *fils*—all are expressions of social criticism and satire or complacent panegyrics proclaiming the moral, intellectual, and artistic progress achieved by these moderns. It is not a great literature, but it is a literature of intense human interest. Its appeal is almost entirely to the intellect, for, except in the case of Rousseau, it fails lamentably when it addresses itself to the emotions. Is there anything more ludicrous and less truly pathetic than a *comédie larmoyante* if it be not a moral tale by Marmontel?

Yet how much more human is the eighteenth century than its august predecessor. Vitality is here the dominant note—vitality and ambition. "We are the moderns," is the cry: "Progress" is the slogan and the goal is liberty—the freedom to write, to speak, to criticise, to worship, to reject the old literary forms and to invent new ones, to cast off the yoke of rational morality and to live by the new sentimental philosophy. The Bastilles erected by tradition to fetter thought bulge and crack ominously. The censorship is gaily eluded. The Sorbonne makes itself a laughing-stock by ordering Buffon to say with his tongue in his cheek that he is in no way infringing the copyright of Moses in his *Histoire naturelle*. The Parlement is forced by Voltaire and by public opinion to revise the cases of Calas and Sirven, the unhappy victims of religious intolerance, and to confess to a miscarriage of justice. The *Encyclopédie*, that vast compendium of what was then the last word in scientific knowledge, carries on the fight against fanaticism and humbug by revealing a new method of approaching truths through the medium of observed facts instead of by the old *a priori* system formulated by Descartes.

But, great as was the achievement of the intellectual giants—the Voltaires, Diderots, Montesquieus, and d'Holbachs—their share in the work of intellectual and social enlightenment was relatively small. A thousand other pens were active in the same cause, and a mass of novels, plays, reflections, satires, and pamphlets, forgotten now but eagerly read by contemporaries, testifies to the influence exercised by these lesser writers. Such a man was the abbé Coyer, and in selecting him as the subject of this study we are under no illusions as to his merits as a stylist or as a thinker. He writes agreeably, like a hundred of his contemporaries; that he has a trenchant wit is no distinction in his century. He is not profound nor is he a prophet. However, for these very reasons he is admirable for the purpose of this essay, which is to offer, if possible, an outline of the social and economic conditions which prevailed in eighteenth-century France. Coyer was an historian, well read in the classics yet critically interested in current events. A scornful critic of contemporary foibles, he was not, however, merely destructive, as his activities in the field of economic reform will show. Without the power to probe deeply into the social questions which he raised, he yet displayed rare judgment and common sense in an age which, both in its clerical and anti-clerical camps, was notoriously intolerant and fanatical.

Gabriel-François Coyer was born at Baumes-les-Dames in 1707. One of thirteen children, brought up in poverty, he had the good luck to attract the attention of the Jesuits, who were always on the look out for talented recruits, though very frequently it was not the Society of Jesus which ultimately profited by this zeal of its teaching fathers. At twenty-four, after the usual thorough grounding in the humanities and in mediaeval philosophy, Coyer became a priest, but five years later, "his love of liberty and of peace," says a contemporary, led him to ask to be relieved of his functions. It is typical of this ex-priest that in a letter to one of his friends exposing his reasons for breaking with the Jesuits he did not, like that ungrateful alumnus, Voltaire, pour obloquy on his former masters. On the contrary, he referred to them in terms of sincere gratitude and admiration.

In 1738 he went to Paris and three years afterwards became tutor to the Prince de Turenne, later Sovereign Duke of Bouillon, in Luxembourg. Through Bouillon's influence and friendship Coyer was appointed Chaplain-General of the Cavalry Corps in 1743, and in this capacity was present at the battle of Lawfeldt and the comic siege of Bergen-op-zoom. Details as to his subsequent movements are meagre, but from a MS. letter we know that he was with the Duke of Bouillon in Navarre in 1759. In 1761 he was received into the *Académie de Nancy* and in 1763 became a member of the *Académie des Arcades*, and two years later, whilst on a visit to England, he was elected Fellow of the Royal Society. He died in 1782, at the age of seventy-five. "His death, like his life, was calm," says his unknown biographer, and indeed, thanks to the protection of the Duke of Bouillon, the abbé seems to have lived happily enough, free from financial cares and respected by many for his sincerity, his modesty, and his patient, laborious existence.

In 1754 Coyer published a number of critical essays on the social life of his time. Their titles indicate the nature of their content: "The Present Century," "The Marvellous Year" (1748), "Pleasures for the People,"

"Letter to a Great Man." These *Bagatelles*, as he called them, caught the fancy of the reading public and acquired for their author a considerable reputation as a shrewd observer of manners.

Coyer attacks what he very sensibly realised to be the cardinal defect of the literature of the eighteenth century—its facility. He sees in the spread of intellectualism a grave threat to the classic ideal of thorough and profound thinking. To him the immense increase in the output of magazines, dictionaries, and almanacs is an indication of the decline of true scholarship, and the rage for literary *salons* and for playgoing but confirms his fears. Coyer, as a son of the people, is a democrat, but his democracy has definite limits which were no doubt marked out during his early training in the Society of Jesus.

Under Louis XIV [he says] it was rather usual for the son of a farmer to till the soil; for the son of an artisan to confine himself to manual labour. To-day they dispute on religion and cut a figure at the Bar. Our agriculture and industry suffer a little, but what does it matter? Intellectualism has taken possession of the State.

What was the real situation? We have only to read the biographies of eighteenth-century men of letters to realise that a great many did indeed belong to the *roture* or non-nobility, but the mass of the people, both peasants and artisans, were almost illiterate, depending as they did for their education on the *écoles de charité*, the existence of which was sporadic and uncertain. But the wealthier *roturiers*, who included the higher and lower bourgeoisie, were able, by sending their sons to the seminaries of the various religious orders, to aliment the liberal professions—medicine, the law, and letters. Yet, as M. Sée points out, the higher bourgeoisie, though exceedingly cultured, constituted but a small section of the total population. As was natural, an educated plebeian usually found his way into the Church, and if he were lucky obtained a curacy, though in the low clergy the level of culture was mediocre and the wretched poverty of the average priest left him with little time or incentive to study. The regular clergy, comprising the various orders, numbered, prior to the reforms of 1766, about twenty-six thousand monks, and, if we believe a contemporary, there were eighty thousand nuns. Orders like the Benedictines, Oratorians, and of course the Jesuits, were justly celebrated for their erudition and in history did valuable research work. It is well known, too, that thousands of these *religieux* were protagonists of the new ideas and contributed largely to the new "philosophic" literature.

Coyer, in his *Bagatelles*, is untiring in his denunciation of the feminist movement which, already evident in the seventeenth century, assumed epidemic proportions in the eighteenth.

Women [he notes] are possessed with the new thirst for knowledge. They dissert, argue, pronounce opinions, and write. . . . The nuns of Port-Royal (the old Jansenist headquarters) used to be considered quite peculiar because they drew up commentaries on the Catechism. To-day *curés* and bishops are at grips with nuns and rich bourgeoises who, newspaper in hand, expound for their benefit the meaning of the Scriptures and the writings of the Fathers.

Coyer, like all publicists who pronounce on the morals of their day, was, however, betrayed into impatient generalisation. Just back from the front after the disastrous War of the Austrian Succession, he found a society in which, as it appeared to him, the sexes were transposed. The young men of the smart set, with their ear-rings, their chat of ribbons, pompoms, and other feminine fal-lals, their tatting and their tapestry-work, their megrims and vapours, aroused the anger of this chaplain of cavalry whose sardonic observations on these *petits messieurs* are worth recording:

Let our surprise cease henceforth, then, to see male individuals in ear-rings doing tapestry-work, receiving in their beds at noon, interrupting a serious conversation to speak to a poodle, talking to their own reflection in the glass, caressing their laces, working themselves into a passion for a broken ornament, falling into a fit over a sick parrot—in short, filching from the other sex all its graces.

The women, on the other hand, alarm him more. " Three things in particular had seemed to distinguish our sex from theirs—to speak little, to think a great deal, and *to rule*." But now he contrasts their silence in the clubs and at church with the ceaseless babble of the little *marquis*. In literature they have abandoned the frivolous trade of novel-writing to men, and history and science hold a greater attraction for these devotees of Newton and Leibniz, whose conversation is centred on serious matters like monads and predestination. Men are now "mere clocks on which women mark the hours—the gambling hour, the hour for the play or the *petit souper*." Young chits of sixteen infatuate men of forty and in the domestic circle husbands are the complacent spectators of their wives' amours. "On va voir *madame*"; "faire la partie de *madame*"; "*madame* est servie," are current expressions which reveal but too well the complete loss of marital authority. The Frenchman who used to indulge in manly games like tennis and pall-mall, now neglects these. He drinks half as much wine as his father and toys with dainty foods, whilst women drink heavily of champagne and liqueurs and think nothing of spending the whole night at a dance in a state of perpetual movement which would prostrate a robust artisan.

Coyer is speaking naturally of the circle he knew, the women of the nobility, or at least of women like Mme Geoffrin, who, if not of the quality, had forced the barriers by money or brains. There were of course more learned ladies, like Mme du Châtelet, whom Coyer doubtless had in mind when he talked of women, with "a sphere in one hand and a compass in the other, measuring and reorganising the universe." Society women flocked to lectures on anatomy and physics and one enthusiast actually travelled with a corpse at the back of her coach for dissection purposes. But outside this limited circle of intellectuals or literary snobs the vast majority of women had little or no opportunity of improving

their culture.   The education offered by the convent
was largely designed to prepare women for the more
trivial aspects of social life.   A smattering of literary
knowledge, *Télémaque*, devotional works, and possibly
Racine's religious tragedies, the ability to write a
model letter, to drop a curtsy, and to strum a sacred
tune, represented the intellectual baggage of the
average *pensionnaire*.   In some of the more fashionable establishments the conversation in the *parloir*
on visiting days was as brilliant as in any *salon*, but
the average mother superior was a woman of limited
imagination and the nuns, though highly estimable
from the point of view of morality, were uninspiring
and little-minded.

About the sixties the wave of sentimentality which
inundated French literature and thought did much
to improve the lot of the Frenchwoman, and writers
like Rousseau attracted thousands of female admirers
who were delighted to find their sex glorified in the
novels and plays of the *âmes sensibles*.   Feminists
like Mme de Graffigny and Mme Lévêque urged the
cause of reform in feminine education, and novelists
like Mme Riccoboni and Marmontel advocated the
abolition of enormities like the forced profession
whereby for purely material reasons girls were virtually hounded into the Church in order to preserve
intact the inheritance of their brothers.   That, however, is a matter upon which Coyer the ex-priest
touches only once, though it is one of the social
abuses most often reflected in the literature of the
century.

A striking feature of the literature of this age is its almost complete silence in regard to the lot of the common people. There are various reasons to explain this apparent apathy. Despite the growing fusion of *roture* and *noblesse*, due to the increasing power of money, the prestige of the Court and old nobility gave rise not so much to a general levelling of the classes as to an insane desire on the part of the middle classes to raise themselves socially by marriage or the purchase of titles. In every stratum of society there was an aristocratic contempt for the under dog. The high clergy, for instance, spoke only in the most arrogant terms of their poorer colleagues the priests and *curés*, and as most of the bishops were noble there was little evidence of Christian charity in this class, the only one where one would expect to find it. The nobility, too, as we shall see, had its Third Estate, whilst in the bourgeoisie, particularly in legal circles, the petty disputes about social precedence provided much amusement for the playgoers or novel-readers of the time. Even in the working classes the same hierarchic differences were strongly marked, and the masters treated their journeymen and apprentices as despotically as they dared.

The literature of the seventeenth century, preoccupied with generalities and abstract ideas, was hardly concerned with man as an individual. Those writers who did offer pictures of the lower orders used them as butts. The eighteenth century, more curious as to the traits which differentiate man from man and one class from another, persisted, however, in displaying the *peuple* as naïve, ludicrous, and gross. Novelists like Marivaux there were, who timidly ran counter to the accepted canons of good taste by offering pictures of the lower middle class in which reality excludes satire, but these were few in number. It was not, indeed, until the advent of the sentimentalists that the people began to figure in the new *drames*, but here truth was sacrificed to a mawkish and whining *sensiblerie* which transformed every peasant into a drivelling idiot or a white-haired old humbug mouthing platitudes about the goodness and generosity of his *bon seigneur*. Coyer, then, interests us because he was one of the first champions of the common man.

In his *Plaisir pour le Peuple* he draws attention to the painful differences existing between citizens of the same estate. One is dressed in velvet, the other in coarse woollen material. Again, we find well-stocked shops whose owners, in their cupidity, would snatch from their poorer fellows the little bread which remains to them after the State has crammed its storehouses. What chance have these wretches, he asks, in the economic battle with no other weapons but their mattocks, their billhooks, and sickles? So they lose. The flower of Coyer's irony, however, is reserved for the *Dissertation on the Nature of the People*, which amazes us by its audacity when we reflect that it was written in 1755.

The author raises the question: "Is the *peuple* composed of human beings?" He touches on the change that has taken place in this class which formerly included farmers, artisans, merchants, financiers, men of letters, and lawyers. Most of these have, however, seceded from the *peuple* which now numbers only peasants, domestic servants, and artisans, whilst even here it is doubtful whether one should include artisans engaged in the luxury trades —jewellers, coach-painters, etc. Philosophers agree, continues Coyer, that it is reason which distinguishes man from the beast, but when he contemplates the dreadful lot of the common people he cannot reconcile their patience with the possession of reason. The common man

lives in a thatched hut or in some hovel allotted to him by our towns because they need his labour. He rises with the sun and, without an upward glance at the fortune which smiles above him, puts on his one suit of clothes, the same for all weathers. He ploughs our fields, he tills our gardens, digs in our mines and quarries, builds houses, and makes our furniture. Hunger comes and everything is the same to him. The day ends and he sleeps on a hard couch in the arms of fatigue. So the animals which we have domesticated, the ox and horse, carry out all the tasks we impose upon them and ask us for nothing but food and shelter. Is this reason?

A reasonable man would ask for gold, silk, perfumes and downy pillows. It is only instinct that is content with mere necessaries. The rational being demands luxury. Instinct keeps people doing in their workshops exactly what they did the day before. Instinct subordinates money to love in marriage.

Have the people any virtues? asks Coyer.

I have never yet read the eulogy of a ploughman any more than I have that of the ox which traces out the furrows along with him. Still, no one will deny that the people has the virtue of patience. . . . It suffers hunger, heat, cold, the insolence of the rich, the brigandage of the tax-collectors, the pillage of the *commis*, and even the ravages of wild animals which it dares not drive away from its crops out of respect for the pleasures of the great.

Contrast the lot of the people with that of the aristocracy. The artisan who is deceived by his wife cannot obtain a separation. He therefore beats her and goes on living with her because she must work. The aristocrat has porters as he has mules. One uses the whip to a restive animal, and where is the gentleman who does not take his stick to a lackey when necessary? Running in front of the carriage of the man of fashion you see a dog and a footman. At the chase there is little difference made between killing a horse or a beater, just as after a battle one does not trouble to publish the names of the private soldiers any more than those of the horses.

But people are beginning to ask themselves how far this state of things can go. "Are we beasts?" is a question frequently overheard among workmen. But they are not beasts, for, says Coyer, they have a human appearance and, moreover, he will undertake to prove that they are human. A celebrated anatomist dissected the skull of a ploughman who hanged himself because for several years, after having paid the King's dues, he had nothing left for himself. In his cranium the surgeon found a number of connected and intelligent ideas on the seasons and the rotation of crops. But the same anatomist, on examining the brain of a nobleman, was unable to discover anything save vague and disjointed perceptions devoid of merit, arrogance mingled with servility, dreams of love and friendship, visions of grandeur, and genealogical chimeras. The proprietor of this skull, by the way, was a gentleman who died sword in hand for having misunderstood a phrase which meant nothing.

Coyer contrasts the complete social and political insignificance of the French common people with the important rôle played by the plebs in republican Rome. Like Voltaire, he draws attention to the English House of Commons, but it should be noted here that Voltaire's attitude towards the *peuple* is the opposite of Coyer's, which is sympathetic and practical. Voltaire had the abstract admiration for democracy which one finds in all intellectuals; he was, however, incapable of entering like Coyer into the mind of the unprivileged classes. In a further article, entitled *De la Prédication*, the abbé continues his attack on the prevailing social system and reviews the so-called moral progress which was the eighteenth century's proudest boast. He questions the value of preaching by examining its results. Whilst Bourdaloue, close on the heels of Bossuet, was fulminating against vice, the Government found itself obliged to erect two tribunals hitherto unknown, one of which was the famous *Chambre ardente* to inquire into the origin of the immense fortunes of the revenue farmers, the other in connection with the sinister *affaire des poisons*. Preaching has no effect on morals, he maintains, not even when it takes the form of literature. Will those who burst into passionate tears at the *Siège de Calais*, he asks, follow the example of the generous citizens portrayed in that play and put their hands in their pockets to relieve the distress of the wretched peasants? "Someone has said that a comedy is an experiment on the human heart. If that is so it resembles many another unsuccessful experiment." Historically, then, one can prove that preaching is a waste of words. What of intellectual progress? A few barbaric prejudices have been removed. The Church has no longer the right to set aside wills by which it does not benefit. The abolition of the right of sanctuary has emptied the churches of murderers. A husband accused of impotence is no longer subjected to the humiliation of a legal examination. Crusades, burning for sorcery or for heresy, have all disappeared; but these are meagre reforms when one considers the deep-seated injustices which disfigure French social life. In Europe crime is rarely punished save when it is committed by the *peuple*. And here Coyer joins hands with the great army of French protagonists of the naturist school of thought. "It is not difficult to prove against Hobbes that man is naturally good. . . . What has made him wicked is the universal scandal of the uselessness of virtue and the prosperity of vice." One has only to look round to find a hundred examples

of inequality. Dancing - masters, jewellers, coach-
painters make more in a day than all the ploughmen
in a province can earn in a month. Matrimony has
become for women a corridor leading to licence. The
triumphant status of the courtesan, the lust for
luxury, the prevalence of debt, debauchery, and
disease, the spectacle of streets and churches swarm-
ing with beggars, the shamefully cynical traffic in
public places, the increase in crime, all point to the
necessity for urgent action by the Government. Coyer
would revive parental powers, re-establish marital
authority, and strengthen the hand of masters in
the various trades so as to set some limit to the
ever-growing number of young men who are attracted
from industry and agriculture into domestic service.
He aims at the establishment of a body of censors
who would handle such breaches of morality as lie
outside the scope of the ordinary laws. The nobility
would no longer enjoy immunity, since in cases of
this kind they could be dealt with by the censors
who would have power to punish by depriving them
of their hereditary titles. The system of taxation,
he thinks, should be altered so that "the *rentiers*,
who merely consume without producing and who
render no service to the State, would be more heavily
mulcted." He attacks the abuses of the existing
legal system, the anomaly of permitting advocates
to plead for or against a case for purely material
considerations, the law's delays, the injustice which
makes it virtually impossible to win a case without
money, the plight of the poor prisoner who cannot

defend himself, the hearing of witnesses in secret, condemnation without unanimity of the jury, and the general corruption of judges.

Turning to economic conditions, he unfolds a truly dreadful picture. The farm labourers, unable to earn a living owing to the demands of the fisc, are obliged to move to the towns in the hope of finding some trade which directly or indirectly caters to the thirst for luxury. The wealthy classes are distinguished by a complete apathy or inhumanity in their relations towards the poor. Child murder is an everyday occurrence, because of the scarcity of institutions for the care of illegitimate children, and even in the Foundling Hospital the mortality is suspiciously high. As for the hospitals for the sick, the conditions are unspeakable: patients suffering from various diseases are huddled together in the same bed and often the dying lie beside the dead. Debtors are taken from useful labour and cast into prison for a trifling sum, whilst the nobility draw a distinction between their debts of honour or gambling debts, which they pay, and their *dettes de justice*, which are never honoured. Trade and agriculture are almost rendered impossible. "The farmer complains of the exactions of the agents of the Treasury; the manufacturer, of the inspections which annoy and oppress him; the artisan, of the corporations which sell him permission to exercise his talents; the invalid soldier, of the assistance which he receives only after it has been diminished by the cupidity of the *traitants*."

In the main, Coyer's summing up of the economic

on account of the dishonesty of millers and vintners who cheated shamelessly on the weights and measures. Toll dues added to the wealth of the seigneur, and although the State now controlled the upkeep of roads and highways, the landlord had still the right to insist on the *corvée* or forced labour of his tenants, though the latter, as a rule, preferred to pay in cash. Generally speaking, the *taille* or income-tax was no longer imposed by the seigneur, this being a Crown privilege. One of the most intolerable of seigneurial rights was that of hunting over tilled ground, and the proper farming of the land was made impossible by the petty game laws laid down by the nobility. Weeds could not be removed till the close of the partridge nesting season, enclosure against the depredations of large and small game was frowned upon or ignored, and the peasants wasted valuable time driving off deer which their landlords did not shoot, either because they were too lazy or more frequently because they were absent, whilst the peasants themselves, of course, were severely dealt with if they poached. In some districts, however, like Brittany, where paternal relations existed between overlord and peasant, fishing and shooting rights were in abeyance. M. Sée indicates that, while there were more peasant farmers than day labourers and farm servants, yet the living conditions of the latter were much harsher than those of the same class in England. Farm servants at the end of the century got from twenty-four to ninety shillings a year in addition to their keep, but the *journaliers* or day labourers had

to eke out a precarious existence on fourpence a day
when they were lucky enough to be in work. "French
common people," says an English newspaper in 1762,
"live on roots and other herbage, four provinces
entirely on chestnuts, and the best of them eat bread
made of barley, millet, turkey, and black corn." Wine
was not within their means, and the ordinary drink
was water or *piquette*, a liquid derived from the lees
of grapes or apples. This is confirmed by modern
researches, and it appears that in periods of famine
the peasant had to eat bread made of fern or bracken
meal. Conditions became worse towards the close
of the century, when the nobility revived many
obsolete seigneurial rights and bled the tenants white,
particularly in the matter of waste lands which had
long been used by farmers for fertiliser in view of
the scarcity of animal manure.

The Crown taxes, the *taille*, the *capitation* or poll-tax,
and the recently introduced *vingtièmes* or twentieths,
together with the *gabelle* or salt-tax, added to the
burden of the common people, though all classes
were supposed to pay the *vingtièmes*. But numerous
offices carried exemption from this imposition, so
that, owing to the opportunities for bribery and
favouritism, the incidence was always on the class
which could least afford to pay. If we add to the above
the indirect taxes on tallow, soap, candles, leather,
linen, and woollen goods we can readily believe the
London Magazine for 1762 which, basing its estimate
on the statements of contemporary French economists, reckons that the Crown taxes alone docked

the labourer of one-third of his earnings in peace time and in time of war of as much as one-half. It is less possible to calculate what percentage was swallowed up by the seigneurial dues, but M. Sée quotes eleven per cent for the Bordeaux district. Again, one must not forget the ecclesiastical tithes which were paid both by nobility and *roture*. Here the peasant again suffered heavily, and if we take the Bordeaux district as a criterion, these *dîmes* accounted for fourteen per cent of a man's earnings.

One of the most iniquitous of seigneurial rights was the so-called *droit de justice*, the abuse of which has been commented on by every eighteenth-century writer of note from Montesquieu to Beaumarchais who, in his *Mariage de Figaro*, has left us an immortal though exaggerated picture of the seigneurial judge. According to his status the seigneur or nobleman had the privilege of dispensing *haute*, *moyenne*, or *basse* justice much in the same way as a present-day army officer can inflict varying sentences according to his rank. But here the analogy ceases, for the eighteenth-century seigneur was represented by a judge whose title varies according to local usage. Generally speaking, he was called the *bailli*, though the names *maire*, *prévôt*, *châtelain*, and *viguier* indicate the same dignitary, who was the most powerful official in the village, as one can well imagine. The seigneur's power was limited to nomination of the judge, since he no longer had, as in the Middle Ages, the right to administer justice personally. Moreover, the qualifications of the judge nominated were examined by the Crown and as a rule these magistrates were capable men and were often upheld by the provincial Parlements against the seigneur where the latter showed himself arbitrary or oppressive. But here again there existed ample opportunities for misconduct, since these magistrates were frequently represented by lieutenants who pandered to the rapacity of overbearing country gentlemen. This explains the enormous numbers of *procureurs, sollici-teurs*, and *notaires* who, of course in return for substantial fees, acted as a further check on seigneurial tyranny. There was also another but more theoretical limitation to the powers of the nobleman, namely the procurator-fiscal, whose duties were ostensibly to watch the interests of both the public and the seigneur as well as of minors. He acted as prosecutor in criminal cases, enforced the collection of seigneurial taxes and of the game laws. In fact he was most frequently the tool or estate agent of the noble landowner, so that he was not noticeably popular with the Third Estate.

But in addition to seigneurial justice the authority of the Crown obtained in a great many districts and in particular where estates or fiefs had once formed part of the royal domains. Certain crimes, too, *cas royaux* like rape, heresy, coining, sedition, etc., could only be tried by the royal courts, and the cunning peasant, if possible, used to build his house on the boundary separating royal from seigneurial jurisdiction. The seigneur could not in the eighteenth century consign an individual to prison without the written authority of the Intendant, the King's most active and powerful representative in his provinces, and frequently the Intendant intervened with salutary effect in cases of wrongful imprisonment or extortion.

Coyer, as a priest, must have been an eyewitness of the appalling hardships suffered by the indigent and the sick in the eighteenth century, for most of the charity work was undertaken by the clergy and the religious orders. One of the great municipal problems, then as now, was the care of the large numbers of unemployed who flocked into the towns from the country districts in bad years. Mendicity was a plague in the reign of Louis XV, despite the brutal measures adopted to punish unauthorised beggars who crowded the churches and public places. Those who received permission to beg from the municipality wore black, yellow, or blue crosses on their shoulders or backs. The others were whipped, branded, or thrown into workhouses when they could be caught. The sick poor were herded in hospitals like Bicêtre, Salpêtrière, and the Hôtel-Dieu where, until the reforms introduced by Louis XVI, patients slept six in a bed and as many as two hundred and seventy were packed into a room. Moreover, there was no attempt to segregate persons suffering from contagious diseases from the others, and criminals of the most revolting type were allowed to contaminate the minds of mere children. Owing to the lack of medical attention conditions were indescribable, particularly in the prisons, which were almost charnel-

induced him to write on a subject so thoroughly in harmony with his liberal and patriotic temper.

In our enlightened times there seems nothing inordinate in the suggestion advanced by the abbé that the nobility should be allowed to engage in commerce, but in 1756 the proposal appeared to thousands revolutionary and scandalous. In the reign of François I, the King, perturbed at the reluctance of noblemen to leave their estates in order to be killed in battle, issued a *loi de dérogeance* to the effect that gentlemen engaging in trade would be deprived of their hereditary titles and privileges. By the eighteenth century, however, the original edict had been amended to permit of noblemen selling the produce of their lands. We know, of course, that during the famous *système* half the French nobility was heavily involved in speculation on the shares of Law's bank and that several of the proudest families trafficked in foodstuffs and amassed disgraceful fortunes. Nevertheless, as a class the nobility could not engage in legitimate commerce without derogation and the only careers open to its sons were still the army, the law, the administration, and the Church. Now, ever since the seventeenth century, the royal traffic in letters of nobility had gone on increasing and the barrier between the bourgeoisie and the aristocracy was lowered to admit the passage of financiers, wealthy merchants, and professional men. Various public offices carried nobility with them, and in the eighteenth century practically all the members of the Parlements or supreme courts were nobles as were the majority of the holders of high municipal posts. The purchase of the estate of a nobleman, which included the enjoyment of seigneurial rights, had the ultimate effect of conferring nobility though a dead-letter law still forbade this. Such abuses were frequent and in outlying districts it was even customary for noblemen to confer on their sons the titles of marquis and chevalier without having taken out a patent. As a result there were as many subdivisions in the *noblesse* as in law and in the Church, ranging from the wealthy and powerful Court and town nobility to the *hobereaux* or country gentlemen whose unhappy plight instigated Coyer to write his *Noblesse commerçante*.

This author estimates the numbers of the nobles of all classes at three hundred and sixty thousand and the provincial nobility at one hundred and eighty thousand, and in the absence of more definite information these figures have been accepted by historians. Coyer points out that the question of creating a trading nobility had been exercising the minds of writers since early in the century. Lassay, usually a bold and subversive author, opposed the admission of the nobility into commerce as likely to deprive the King of officers in time of war, an argument which Coyer disposes of summarily by showing that, even if the army were at its maximum war establishment, it could not absorb more than thirty thousand officers. He emphasises the unfortunate situation of the thousands of poor country noblemen who are obliged to starve on their tiny estates in deference to a stupid decree which can no longer be justified either from the point of view of necessity or of honour. Like Voltaire, he turns to England, where trade is not only held in high esteem but attracts members of the oldest families. Picture, he says, the condition of the indigent French nobility.

Let us follow them to their homes: let us explore with them those seigneurial lands which cannot support their seigneurs. See those farms without cattle, those badly cultivated fields and those which lie fallow, those miserable crops which a creditor is awaiting, writ in hand, that château which threatens to collapse on its master, that uneducated, ill-clad family, a father and mother united by the common bond of tears.

He is not exaggerating, for we learn from other contemporaries that eight hundred francs was an average annual income for an *hobereau*, who also had frequently to save out of this sum the amount necessary to purchase a commission for his eldest son. It is this poverty which explains the growing insolence in the attitude of wealthy farmers towards the local squire and the many appeals to the Intendant for disciplinary action against these mutinous *roturiers*. One agrees with Coyer when he indicates the futility of possessing the seigneurial privilege to hunt or to occupy a special pew in church under such circumstances. Even the *droit de justice* was an empty distinction where the law, as it was prone to do, favoured the more wealthy litigant.

Compared with the English country gentry, of whom at least six thousand had an annual income of ten thousand francs, the *hobereau* cut a sorry figure. Inevitably his lands, heavily mortgaged, reverted to wealthy nobles or, worse still, to financiers who acquired rank in this fashion. "I am not going to discuss the question as to whether new men who rise by industry are not more estimable than the old nobles who have fallen into idleness," says Coyer, who, it is clear, would not have shed a tear if the whole *noblesse* had ceased to exist. What perturbs him as a patriot is the social evil represented by the presence of thousands of idlers at a critical moment in the history of his country. England, he points out, is casting covetous eyes on the French colonies, and he fears a nation "which thinks like ancient Rome and trades like Carthage." In time of peace the French nobility is "an inactive, immobile, and paralytic corps." In despair at not getting commissions in their own army many gentlemen take service with foreign regiments. Even those who are lucky enough to obtain a post at home know that they can never marry, whilst lack of capital prevents them from exploiting their estates. Twenty-five million acres lie fallow for this reason which is the direct cause of the distress of the peasant crofter. The proof is that near towns where business men invest money in farms, conditions are vastly different.

The question of depopulation is, according to Coyer, intimately connected with the situation just exposed. The poor nobility find it cheaper to put their land into pasture rather than into crops, and the resulting unemployment among the peasant class has driven

them to practise birth control or not to marry at all.
The younger sons of country noblemen accept curacies
or join the celibate Order of Malta, and their daughters,
having no dowry, are obliged to take the veil. Others,
like the unemployed peasants, move to the large
towns where too often they swell the numbers of
criminals who infest the capital. The poor provincial nobility are not even consumers of French
products and imports. "It is not for them that
Abbeville makes cloth, Lyons silkstuffs, Valenciennes
laces, Beauvais its tapestries, and Paris its mirrors and
fashions. It is not for them that our colonies grow
coffee, cocoa, sugar, and cotton. The English and
Dutch peasants consume all these and are better
clothed and fed than they."

Coyer belongs to the mercantilist school of economic
thought, and for him the future of France lay in the
increase of her colonial trade.   In reply to those who
still hankered after legendary gold mines as a source
of revenue, a dream which even the Law disaster
had not eradicated, he replies: "Do not let us covet
the mines of Peru; those who showed them to M. de
La Condamine had no shoes to their feet. Great
commerce is the richest of all mines." He points to
the prosperity of England, with her merchant fleet
of ten thousand ships and one hundred and fifty
thousand men; of Holland, to whom France in three
years alone paid one and a half millions for the mere
freightage of vessels bringing naval ammunition to
her ports. With an increased mercantile fleet, un-
exploited colonies like San Domingo, Cayenne, and

Louisiana could be made as productive as Canada and the Windward Islands and piracy stamped out by armed trading vessels. And yet, exclaims Coyer, there are people who ask: "What shall we do with our nobility?" Can they not enter the mercantile marine and thus form a valuable nursery for the navy? Is it more honourable to sell wine, corn, and cattle or to act as page or squire to the *haute noblesse* than to engage in foreign trade? Yet such is the absurd prejudice against commerce in France that she has not even a ministry of trade. Whilst England is represented abroad by business men like Falkner and Keene, France is content to send as ambassadors incompetents who have nothing to recommend them save their lineage and titles. Just imagine, says the abbé, a comte Samuel Bernard! He is referring to the millionaire financier who lent money to Louis XIV, but who could not be ennobled on account of the prejudice against commerce. In England he would have been honoured by his sovereign.

Already Voltaire, in his *Lettres philosophiques*, had employed his pen in the defence of commerce and also dedicated his tragedy, *Zaïre*, to his friend Falkner, the business man who represented England at Constantinople. It is, however, typical of Voltaire that, in a letter to de Servan in 1766, he sneeringly refers to Coyer as the man "who wanted to put the Montmorencies and Châtillons into shops." The explanation is that the abbé, though at one time hailed as "one of our brothers," had fallen foul of the *philosophes.* A well-known anecdote indicates 1761 as the probable date of the rupture which was pre-cipitated by Voltaire's malicious *mot.* Coyer had gone to Ferney and expressed his intention of staying six weeks. "Ah! monsieur l'abbé," said his host, "surely you don't want to resemble Don Quixote. He mistook inns for castles: you mistake castles for inns." Poor Coyer was at that moment on an obligatory journey recommended by the Lieutenant of Police as a result of his *History of Sobieski* which was too outspoken on religious and political matters. Besides, Voltaire, himself a parvenu noble, had no desire to see the ranks of the *noblesse* swelled by ennobled merchants. Like most of the opponents of Coyer's scheme, therefore, he sought to kill it by ridicule. A cartoon appeared showing a nobleman, yard-stick in hand, folding cloth and lifting bales under the direction of a gross plebeian. "Those who despise trade," retorted Coyer, "laugh at fictions of their own invention, whereas I laugh at sights which are really ridiculous, at men who are proud of being beggars and who, provided they may be idle, are not ashamed to cringe, fawn, and flatter for a mean and miserable livelihood."

Eighteenth-century readers of the *Noblesse com-merçante* rightly discerned beneath the immediate issue raised by the author a deliberate attack on the existing social hierarchy. Only in this way can one understand the long and bitter polemic provoked by this book which set bourgeoisie and nobility by the ears, emphasising the gulf that separated these two

classes. The result was to exacerbate old grievances
and to create a state of mind which partly explains
the renewed harshness displayed by large sections of
the nobility who in the years preceding the Revolution revived seigneurial rights which had fallen into
abeyance and, usually by illegal methods, deprived
the tenantry of the use of heath and wood lands which
they had long been accustomed to regard as their
property.

The most violent opposition to Coyer's scheme came
of course from the military nobility, who had special
grounds for apprehension. A fiery soldier of the "Die-
hard" school, the chevalier d'Arcq, was the self-
appointed spokesman of the army caste, and in his
provocative *Noblesse militaire* he advanced to the
attack. On general principles, he maintained, the
institution of a commercial nobility was unthinkable
since the object of commerce is self-interest, which
is fundamentally opposed to the ideals of an officer
and gentleman—honour, patriotism, and self-sacrifice.
Commerce, therefore, cannot be ennobled. Again,
admitting that considerable fusion had already taken
place between the Third Estate and the nobility,
d'Arcq foresaw no good to the State from an aggra-
vation of this undesirable intermingling of the social
orders. The creation of a commercial nobility, he
continued, would upset "the harmonious inequality
of the classes," a delightful phrase which expresses
better than could volumes the naïve arrogance of
the *noblesse d'épée*. For the chevalier there is only
one profession fit for a gentleman—the army, and

he fears that if this new and lucrative outlet were offered to the nobility the army would be deprived of the right type of officer. It is irrelevant, he said, to argue like Coyer that the nobility has already such an outlet in the Church, though it does not avail itself of it to any great extent. The clerical profession is not attractive because it has few plums to offer, and these are for the most part reserved for the most powerful houses or for the Court favourites.

D'Arcq now touches on the real grievance of his caste, the granting of commissions to *roturiers*, an abuse, he says, which has its roots in the venality of officials, in the *concordats* or military confederations, and in the corps commanders' right of nomination to lesser posts. In reply to Coyer's objection that the army even at full strength could absorb but a relatively small number of officers, the author of the *Noblesse militaire* advocates an increase in the establishment of infantry and cavalry, a revival of the old system of having seconds in command of regiments, and the creation of a volunteer corps consisting entirely of nobles who would thus no longer be reduced to the indignity of accepting minor posts as clerks in the Treasury.

In discussing the decline of French military power in the eighteenth century historians overlook one serious source of disintegration, namely the diminishing *moral* of the army, some of the reasons for which have been outlined by d'Arcq. The majority of officers still belonged to the nobility, but both Louis XIV and his grandson were anxious to attract

the moneyed bourgeoisie to the profession of arms.
There were various reasons for this. A colonel was
the proprietor of his regiment and received his commission only on condition that he kept it up to
strength, and a company commander in peace time
was expected to bring back at least two recruits on
his return from his quarterly furlough. In cases
where the officer was a wealthy and influential landowner he had no difficulty in attracting men who
knew that in their absence their families would be
well looked after. Others had recourse to *racoleurs*
or professional recruiting officers, some of whom were
subalterns in need of money, though frequently the
work was done by civilians or private soldiers. Until
1760, and even after, in spite of a law passed to
limit their activities, *racoleurs* resorted to every
kind of trick to engage men. The ignorant rustics,
attracted by wonderful but lying tales of sumptuous
food, unlimited wine and money, fell an easy prey to
these sharks, who usually enlisted their dupes after
having first made them stupid with liquor. Again,
the reckless extravagance of the general officers, who
were chosen from the highest nobility, set up a standard of living that very few of the lesser nobles could
afford to imitate, while there was no lack of wealthy
commoners eager to fill their places since personal
or military nobility was conferred for long and
meritorious service in the commissioned ranks. In
certain crack regiments, however, like the Guards,
the Light Horse Guards, or the Musketeers, which
composed the King's Household (*La Maison du Roi*),

proof of nobility was required of all aspirant officers. An army order of 1749, reducing the number of battalions to one hundred and sixty-eight, inflicted great hardship on the poor junior officers, hundreds of whom were demobilised and reduced to beggary, whilst lads of seventeen were granted colonelcies merely because of their lineage. Again, a French officer who had not the means to keep up an establishment was obliged to spend his life in billets, for all troops were quartered on the civilian population who of course detested them, usually with good reason. In addition to the regular army which was theoretically recruited by voluntary enlistment, every district contributed a battalion to the militia, whose members were drawn by lot. Only the working classes were liable for this service and, as married men were exempt, hurried and ill-assorted marriages such as were common in Great Britain during the recent war, frequently occurred in eighteenth-century France when the lots were drawn. In the circumstances, then, it is not surprising that the army failed to live up to the glorious achievements of the previous era.

With soldierly contempt for civilian matters like the advancement of French overseas trade and the problem of depopulation, d'Arcq dismisses these questions with a wave of the hand. French commerce is getting on very well as it is. Indeed the country has reached the limits of her trading capacity, as is evidenced by the fact that the *Compagnie des Indes* is over-staffed. As for depopula-

tion, let the Government offer financial inducements
to the peasant farmer by granting him exemption
from the *taille* when he breaks in fallow land or otherwise merits reward. As for agrarian crises, let the
Crown erect storehouses, forbid the export of grain,
and hoard wheat in good years against periods of
famine. In this way the peasants would be attracted
back to the land and there would be no depopulation
problem. The chevalier d'Arcq, in these suggestions,
was echoing the views of economists like de Gournay,
Turgot, and others who believed that the economic
salvation of France lay not in an increase of her
overseas trade but in agricultural reforms. Thanks
to their efforts, in the thirty years preceding the
Revolution much was done to improve agrarian
conditions. Exemption from the *taille* for four years
was granted to peasant farmers who broke in fallow
land. Intendants were instructed to indemnify
farmers whose crops were damaged by storm or
by animals; seed grain was imported, potato-growing
encouraged, and nurseries of mulberry-trees established by the Government. Attempts were made to
improve the quality of horses and cattle by the
creation of stud-farms and for the first time statistics
of crops and animals were officially prepared. To
prevent famine the State bought up grain, offered
subventions to growers, and forbade the exportation
of wheat from certain districts and enforced its sale
in others, confiscating ruthlessly where there was
any suspicion of hoarding for speculation purposes.
Everything, in short, was done save to remove the

real source of trouble, which was the seigneurial regime.

Mme Belot, a shrewd and fearless writer, whilst agreeing with d'Arcq that it would be dangerous to tamper with the hierarchic system, supported Coyer in his attack on the luxurious mode of life of the moneyed classes, noble and bourgeois.

If our seigneurs [said this lady], instead of selling their estates to gamble at Court exploited them properly; if they did not ruin their horses in sumptuous carriages instead of putting them out to plough; if the eldest sons would live on sixty thousand francs instead of one hundred thousand when their income is eighty thousand; if they did not abandon their younger brothers; if they did not depopulate the provinces of ploughmen for domestic service; if they would protect the impoverished nobility, the down-trodden peasant, and the industrious artisan instead of lavishing money on opera actresses; if they did without crystal dinner-services when at war or gave one hundred crowns salary to their sons' tutor as willingly as they give fifty louis to their coachman; if they reduced the number of their servants and suppressed gold lace on clothes; if the bourgeoisie would do without diamonds and cloth of gold; if the flower-girls gave up their silver plate and mantlets; if in every class one was not the ox for those below and the frog to those above, the nobility would be better off and domestic trade better understood. There would be more recruits for the army and navy and plenty of farm labourers because people would be released from the luxury trades.

Mme Belot, d'Arcq, Coyer, and indeed all the participants in this polemic unite in condemning the passion for luxury which in the eighteenth century

was in reality mere movement, and retrogressive movement at that. The spiritual elements in life and in literature made way for immorality, cynicism, and superficiality. The serious things of life, the new and pregnant ideas of tolerance, humanitarianism, and in general the whole philosophic propaganda of the age were expressed in a witty and flippant tone in deference to the reigning mode. *L'esprit* was the first essential in a writer, were he poet, philosopher, or scientist. Fontenelle and Voltaire were adepts in this manner. Of Montesquieu's *Esprit des Lois* Mme du Deffand could say with some truth that it was "De l'esprit sur les Lois," and even the solemn Buffon essays a sprightly caper in his *Natural History*.

Small wonder, then, that the great mass of the wealthy and non-intellectual found an easy outlet for their expressionism in gorgeous clothing, magnificent *soupers*, colourful theatrical entertainments, sensual pictures and books, exotic gardens, and beautifully decorated mansions. At the Court of Louis the Well-Beloved gambling and debauchery consumed large fortunes. We have only to read the secret reports of the inspectors of the Paris police to realise that the royal example was followed by hundreds of the nobility. Harems, established after the model of Louis's infamous *Parc aux Cerfs* at Versailles, cost their princely owners incredible sums and excited the cupidity and immorality of the women of the people. The attitude of the upper classes was, if anything, worse, for the nobility condemned the *Parc aux Cerfs* not on moral grounds but simply because Louis had the bad taste to prefer the daughters of the people to their own who were metaphorically thrown at his head. Mme Belot suggests, as do others, that the craze for luxury had penetrated to the lower classes, and this was true of the large towns where artisans and shopkeepers catering to the extravagance of the rich became inevitably infected by the desire to ape their betters. The servant class was obviously the first to be debauched by the bad example set by the nobility and rich bourgeois, many of whom kept staffs of thirty or forty valets, not to speak of maids, cooks, coachmen, gardeners, and other domestics. One of Coyer's opponents in the *Noblesse militaire et commerçante* drew attention to the fact that Paris in 1756, with a population of a million, contained sixty thousand servants "who by virtue of their calling were reduced to a sort of celibacy." One realises, therefore, the force of Mme Belot's reference to the depopulation of the provinces of ploughmen for domestic service.

The same writer, by way of contrast, offers a picture of the miserable lot of the peasant:

I see in the country a thatched cottage almost torn down by the winds. Joy never strays into this frightful dwelling. Gloomy and difficult of approach, its mournful silence is broken only by the moans of its inmates who cry out from the depths of their grief: "Shall we then bring more unhappy wretches into the world!"

But the situation of the peasantry, numerically and economically the most important class in France, had no need of such sentimental exaggeration. By

1760 conditions had become so bad that palliative remedies such as those suggested by Coyer and other publicists could do little more than touch the surface of the evil which was the legalised exploitation of the agricultural labourer and small farmer by an idle and privileged caste.   This explains why even the sound, economic reforms of the Government of Louis XVI were of little avail, stultified as they were by the renaissance of seigneurial rapacity and oppression which characterised the twenty years preceding the Revolution.   It cannot be said, however, that the efforts of men like Coyer were entirely fruitless: every unselfish gesture carries civilisation forward.   And at a time when it required no little courage to plead the cause of the unprivileged, situated in circumstances very conducive to that moral cowardice we call apathy, the abbé Coyer generously dedicated his talents to the work of social reform.   When at last Death touched him on the shoulder he was quietly working at a definitive edition of the writings to which he had consecrated a long and full life.

VOLTAIRE'S GREATEST ENEMY

FEW great men of letters possessed Voltaire's capacity for intense and tenacious hatred: few, too, cultivated to such a fine degree the art of making enemies and of keeping them. The *Contes* and the vast *Correspondance* owe their sempiternal vivacity to Voltaire's fermenting amour-propre, his merciless irony, and his cruel intolerance of ideas or sentiments which displeased him. The passion of hatred, which in the ordinary man temporarily impairs the intellectual functions, became in the case of Arouet a source of inspiration, stimulating his power of expression and lending to his style that individual, indefinable charm which we call Voltairian. Essentially a polemist, for he lacked the creative gift of the great dramatist, Voltaire's principal medium was satire, in every form of which, ranging from the foulest abuse to the noblest invective, he was a consummate artist. No opponent, however petty, escaped his watchful and tremendous vanity, and the index to his correspondence teems with the names of tenth-rate scribblers of whom not even Voltaire's contemporaries would have been aware had not he himself dragged them from the obscurity which was their normal *milieu*. But perhaps Arouet's greatest achievement was the fabrication of the legend of an infallible and fearless Voltaire fighting a magnificent battle for the truth against a legion of sinister foes. Time has consolidated this myth in which he appears as a sort of intellectual Jack the Giant-Killer, and ogres like Desfontaines, Fréron, and La Beaumelle who dared to pit their incredible stupidity against the lambent wit of the Sage of Ferney are invariably baffled, confounded, and conspued. It is true that literary historians have tried to correct this romantic illusion by adducing facts to show that to have been an enemy of Voltaire's is not necessarily a symptom of cretinism. But the education of public opinion is a slow process, and the average Frenchman clings to his conception of Voltaire the paladin of liberty, the flail of superstition, and the protagonist of humanitarianism. Only one of Arouet's enemies has escaped the popular fate—Piron, the Burgundian playwright, and he owes his immunity to his redoubtable wit and his rare sense of humour. The most fanatical of Voltairians was forced to respect a man who celebrated his failure to enter the French Academy in the following immortal epigram:

> Ci-gît Piron qui ne fut rien,
> Pas même académicien.

Of all Voltaire's enemies Élie-Catherine Fréron is undoubtedly the man whose reputation has been most unjustly distorted by posterity. Nisard and Cornou have done much to rehabilitate him though in different ways. Thus, Fréron emerges from Nisard's apologia with scarcely a shred of moral character but cleared of the accusation of stupidity, whilst according to M. Cornou, who is an honorary canon of Quimper, he is a paragon of virtue and a much-persecuted defender of the faith. The truth seems to be somewhere between these two opinions and not very far from that advanced by M. Cornou.

The Voltaire-Fréron quarrel which we are about to describe is immediately interesting because it reveals aspects of Voltaire's character that lie outside the scope of a general biography. But its real significance will be found in the great conflict of ideas of which the quarrel is merely an incident—in the famous battle which the forces of tradition represented by Fréron and the Church waged against the activities of the *philosophes* or freethinkers supported by Voltaire. It would be difficult to exaggerate the import of this struggle, the results of which can be detected in the present organisation of French society, for the Revolution of 1789 cannot in any sense be regarded as having decided the issues raised in 1750, which is usually looked upon as the date of the outbreak of hostilities.

We have seen that as early as the close of the seventeenth century Bayle and the *libertins* had done much to sap the old beliefs and that Voltaire as a young man was closely identified with the new movement. His *Lettres philosophiques* marked him as the Moses who was to lead the children of the new faith into the promised land of liberty and fraternity, for as yet equality had not been indicated as the third member of the trinity in this new godhead. By 1748

Arouet was easily the most important figure in the
literature of western Europe, in correspondence with
the savants of England, Holland, and Germany and
a familiar of princes and noblemen both French
and foreign.   Royal Historiographer, Member of the
Académie française and Gentleman of the King's Bedchamber, lately returned from a not very important
but highly flattering diplomatic mission to Prussia,
and a protégé of the fickle Mme de Pompadour,
it seemed as if even a Voltaire's insatiable desire
for glory must be at last assuaged.   But he was
constitutionally unable to leave well alone.   The
same vulgarity and lack of tact which made him
turn to M. de Richelieu at the performance of his
Temple de la Gloire and ask fatuously in the King's
hearing: "Trajan est-il content?" produced the celebrated *gaffe* of the madrigal to Mme de Pompadour
with its equivocal eulogy coupling the names of
mistress and monarch in the most public fashion:

> Que vos jours précieux soient marqués par des fêtes!
> Que la paix dans nos champs revienne avec Louis!
> Soyez tous deux sans ennemis
> Et tous deux *gardez vos conquêtes.*

Court society shrugged its shoulders and raised ex-
pressive eyebrows.   Pompadour, furious, transferred
her protection to the aged Crébillon and the tactless
rhymester received instructions from the Lieutenant-
General of Police to remove himself to the country.
So Arouet petulantly betook himself to Cirey to con-
sole himself in the company of the mathematical but
amorous Mme du Châtelet and to toy with the idea

of accepting the flattering invitations of Frederick
to go to Berlin as chamberlain, literary adviser, and
philosophic companion to. His Prussian Majesty.

Fréron's career up to this point, though less spectacular than Voltaire's, yet provides an interesting
commentary on the trials of a literary critic in an
age when journalism was a new and precarious way
of earning a livelihood. Born at Quimper in 1718,
Fréron became a distinguished pupil of the Jesuits,
who found him a post as *professeur de cinquième* at
the famous college of Louis-le-Grand.   But already
the obligations which the Church imposes on her
novices were beginning to weigh irksomely upon the
ardent temperament of the Breton Fréron, who was
better fitted for the stormy career of letters than for
the safe but uneventful business of schoolmastering.
His intercourse with the great humanist, *père* Brumoy,
a fervent admirer and friend of the poet Jean-Baptiste Rousseau, stimulated Fréron's literary ambitions,
and whilst he was still a student of rhetoric the good-
natured Brumoy entrusted his eager neophyte with
the correction of a MS. poem passed on to him by
Jean-Baptiste, whose reputation as the greatest living
French poet rankled in Voltaire's mind like a sore.
It was almost inevitable, then, that Fréron should
abandon all idea of the priesthood. He had been
barely two years at Louis-le-Grand when some zealous
delator espied the novice at the theatre in lay attire.
As a disciplinary measure Fréron was deprived of his
post and sent to Alençon where his request to be
relieved of his vows was granted.   So, his conscience

freed of an intolerable burden, the ex-priest of twenty-
one joyously devoted himself to the difficult trade of
making a living as an arbiter of literary taste. There
was nothing yet to distinguish this young abbé from
a hundred other wearers of the *petit collet* save that
Fréron was not of the breed, then so common, which
picked up an odd crown or an occasional commen-
datory benefice by lounging in ladies' boudoirs.

A vacancy occurred on the staff of the critical
review, *Observations sur les Écrits modernes*. It
was offered to Fréron, who eagerly grasped the
opportunity of receiving an invaluable course in
training under the editor, Desfontaines, a writer of
experience, an ardent humanist, and a bitter enemy
of Voltaire's. When, in 1740, the apprentice assumed
his functions Paris was still echoing with the noise
of Arouet's venomous campaign against Desfontaines's
Voltairomanie, a pitiless exposure of Voltaire's weak-
nesses containing a stinging reference to a certain
thrashing inflicted on the great man by the poet
Beauregard. Theoretically, as usual, Voltaire had
justice on his side, for the *Voltairomanie* was the
reply to a pamphlet not actually written by Voltaire
but by his *âme damnée* and *chef de cabale*, the chevalier
de Mouhy. However, Desfontaines, who had, as they
say, "beak and claws," was not disposed to waste
time in idle and pedantic discrimination. Voltaire's
rage was indescribable. He bombarded all his friends
with importunate letters urging them to move heaven
and earth to have Desfontaines thrown into jail and
the *Observations* suppressed. "There is no middle

way," he wrote feverishly to Thieriot in 1739.   "I am
dishonoured if Desfontaines' libel is not replied to, if
this infamous calumny is not confounded.   The tears
stream from my eyes as I write to you.   In God's
name run to *père* Brumoy.   See some of the fathers,
my old masters, who can never be my enemies. Speak
to them tenderly, forcibly. . . ." The "old masters"
were curiously unmoved by the touching plight of their
distinguished alumnus, who tried successively to enlist
the aid of the police, the Court, and the Parlement
in his attack on the "vilain prêtre" Desfontaines, to
quote the most innocuous of Arouet's epithets which
astonish us by their violence until we happen to
stumble on the following illuminating sentence in one
of his letters: "A man's reputation with posterity,"
says Voltaire in reference to the *Voltairomanie*, "is
written on the authority of such memoirs."   But
Arouet was historian enough to know that history
is not an epitome of irresponsible or malicious
calumnies. The sting to his amour-propre lay in
the fact that the *Voltairomanie* was essentially true.
The reference to the verdict of posterity has a fine
air of dignified detachment: coming from a man in
the autumn of life it would be touching in its nobility;
but Voltaire was forty-five and in the flower of his
intellectual vigour.   The only opinion he cared about
was that of his contemporaries who, as he knew
better than anyone, eagerly welcomed facts of the
kind so indiscreetly revealed by his enemy.

Into this welter of journalistic storm and stress
came Fréron, who can therefore be said to have

assumed as one of the functions of his office a sort of moral obligation to defend the cause of Desfontaines. To his honour as a critic it must be pointed out that he did not, like his chief, allow his personal prejudices to affect his literary judgment of Voltaire's works. On the death of Desfontaines he did, however, pay grateful homage to his former master's kindness and to the gentleness and affability of his private life. In a passage obviously addressed to Voltaire he excused his late friend's lapses from that exact impartiality which Fréron himself ever tried to hold before his mind as the ideal of the literary critic.

All decent people have observed with indignation [he wrote] that he (Desfontaines) was the victim of an odious cabal whilst the most pitiful creatures were overwhelmed with literary honours.

> *Ploravere suis non respondere favorem*
> *Speratum meritis.*

It must be admitted that our abbé was born with sentiments. A philosopher in his conduct as in his principles, he was free from ambition; he had in his mind a noble pride which would not allow him to stoop to solicit benefits or titles.

Articles of this kind were scarcely calculated to endear Fréron to Arouet, whose vanity did not blind him to the satire lurking beneath every phrase of the eulogy on his deceased enemy. But this was not his only grievance against Fréron, who had dared to poke fun at Voltaire's infatuation for Newton in a passage closing with the lines:

Voltaire, tu naquis pour peindre la nature,
Est-ce à toi de la mesurer?

Now, to the casual observer there was nothing but sound and friendly advice in the implication that Voltaire the great poet would be better employed in consecrating his talents to the Muses than "in tracing sterile lines with the compass of Newton." And did not Fréron in another passage refer to him as the peer of Tasso, of Milton, and of Virgil? But to understand Voltaire's chagrin one must realise his actual situation at this moment. Engaged in feverish intrigues to enter the French Academy, the poet-dramatist knew that he must make his peace with the Church if his candidature was to have any useful support. His orthodoxy was, to put it mildly, suspect, and all Arouet's activities were therefore directed towards the removal of this annoying impression. Newton's rôle in this imbroglio will be discerned in the opening passage of a humble letter addressed to the members of the Academy:

I have the honour to send you the proofs of a second edition of the *Elements of Newton* in which I have given an abstract of his metaphysics. I address this homage to you as judges of the truth. You will see that Newton was, of all the philosophers, the most persuaded of the existence of God and that I was right in saying that a catechist announces God to his children and a Newton demonstrates Him to wise men. . . .

The victory of Fontenoy in 1745 afforded Voltaire another opportunity of pressing his claims, this time with the Court. But again the pestilential Fréron ruined the success of his scheme by writing an ode which was pronounced by competent judges to be superior to Voltaire's hurried *Poème de Fontenoy*.

In 1745, Fréron, already favourably known by verses which though of no great merit were better than most of the stuff that passed as poetry in this prosaic age, and encouraged by the success of his critical pieces, founded a review called *Les Lettres de la Comtesse*. Here, under the veil of an anonymity tacitly approved by the censorship, he surveyed the state of contemporary literature and in malicious, sparkling prose passed judgment on Piron, Fontenelle, and, of course, on Voltaire, the "Alexander of letters." The bogus Comtesse paid homage to the latter's talents but expressed surprise that his literary reputation should be a subject of argument.

Some, admiring the fertility of his pen, condemn his inconstancy. For myself, I confess, I cannot find it in me to blame his avidity for every sort of glory; and as he is the greatest poet of our day I feel disposed to excuse him for wanting to be historian, philosopher, geometer, physicist, tragedian, comic author, lyricist, politician—in short, everything. It is only feeble and timid souls who regard as madness the noble ambition to conquer the whole world which devoured Alexander.

As this equivocal eulogy progresses there emerges a picture of Voltaire which must have been extremely galling to his amour-propre, the picture of a *homme universel*, a Jack-of-all-trades, the Gil Blas of letters. And there was more than a grain of truth in Fréron's malicious criticism. Dropping all pretence of frivolity, the author indicated two of Arouet's serious defects, first, the absence of continuity in his ideas, which was but ill-compensated for by the force and colour of his expression, and secondly, the lack of that creative power which distinguishes the work of a genius like Racine.

Reverting to his original manner, Fréron then pretended to defend Voltaire against current reproaches of egotism, interested generosity, and overweening vanity. In reply to an imaginary assertion that Voltaire's star was waning, he wrote:

> Has he not the prerogative of heroes, who by the multitude of their great achievements have earned the right to deteriorate? Although our poet has not yet been ushered into the privileged temple of the immortal *beaux esprits*, his brilliant successes and his numerous laurels assuredly give him the right henceforth to produce indifferent writings. . . .

The memory of Desfontaines was avenged; but Fréron, carried away by the spirit of badinage, brought down on his head the wrath of Mme de Pompadour by a scathing reference to a protégé of hers, the fashionable but shallow poet Bernis. A brief sojourn at Vincennes taught Fréron a lesson in discretion. In a rueful but witty letter to the head of the censorship he pointed out gently that though poets are proverbially fond of solitude it is not the solitude of a fortress like Vincennes, adding as an earnest of his penitence:

> Il n'est rien que je ne promette
> Pour sortir de ce triste lieu.
> Ma muse, désormais discrète,
> Résistera (s'il plaît à Dieu)

A la démangeaison secrète
De turlupiner les écrits
Que la sottise dans Paris
Enfante, distribue, achète. . . .

This "secret itch" was a constant source of trouble to Fréron, who did not belong to the fortunate but uninteresting category of those who suffer fools gladly, and the Vincennes episode was by no means destined to be his only skirmish with the authorities.

Voltaire remained silent under the provocative attacks of the Comtesse. Sedulously employed in the delicate business of currying favour with the Church, on which depended the success of his candidature to the Academy, he was not the man to embroil himself in a quarrel the outcome of which could only mean unwelcome publicity at a moment when he was posing as the sage of Christendom. Besides, the imprisonment of Fréron and the consequent suppression of *Les Lettres de la Comtesse* acted as a magic salve to his irritated amour-propre. His obvious course then was to lie low until after his election when he would be free to turn upon his enemies with that concentrated ferocity which comes from rancour long suppressed. Meanwhile Fréron, an exile at Bar-sur-Seine—he had not yet received permission to return to Paris—heard doubtless through his old masters of Voltaire's unctuous letter to *père* de La Tour in which Arouet with revolting cynicism humbly protested his undying affection for the Jesuits and his fidelity to the Catholic cause. Voltaire was elected, and his speech elicited from Fréron an ironical commentary

better of Fréron in the field of criticism, insulted him in public and a duel, for which, by the way, neither combatant had any stomach, was happily frustrated by the police to the secret relief of both parties. An anonymous eulogy of Voltaire's works written by Voltaire himself gave Fréron a chance to practise his new system of attack. Feigning to believe in the authenticity of the work, he expressed deep concern that the reputation of a great poet should be thus exposed to ridicule by a well-meaning but indiscreet eulogist. It must be extremely annoying, he suggested, for an author of Voltaire's notorious modesty and reticence to find himself lauded to the skies to the detriment of a number of his eminent contemporaries whose works were unjustly and stupidly criticised by the anonymous panegyrist. "If I were Monsieur de Voltaire," continued Fréron with mock sincerity, "I should make every effort to discover the seditious author of a libel in which he is so clumsily flattered." Voltaire, unable to reply immediately and for obvious reasons, bided his time and then launched a virulent attack against the deceased Desfontaines and all journalists who "insult their fellow-men for gain." Fréron replied on behalf of his dead friend and in an astronomical fantasy compared Voltaire to a heavenly body, covered with many spots, revolving erratically round Parnassus, accompanied by its satellites. Passing to a serious estimate of Voltaire's position in French literature, he praised his wit, his grace, and the vivacious colouring of his style. "I do not say," he concluded with remarkable foresight, "that his writings will not go down to posterity, but I doubt if posterity will place him in the same rank as the great geniuses of last century. He will be read as a writer of great wit who was lacking in essential parts. It is invention and judgment which make great poets." Now, Fréron was in a precarious position. His permission to print anonymously under a foreign imprimatur rested on a mere verbal tolerance. Voltaire, after a little difficulty it is true, managed to obtain the suppression of the *Lettres*, and to achieve this he did not hesitate to use his influence as a member of the Academy. Not content with taking away Fréron's livelihood, he dissuaded Frederick the Great from appointing the critic as his literary correspondent by representing him as a man who had been in prison "for rather ugly reasons" and as a person whose acquaintance would be compromising if not dishonourable. It is typical of Arouet that at this very moment he was making overtures to his victim through his niece, Mme Denis, who twice invited him to a private performance of Voltaire's *Rome sauvée*, an invitation which was twice refused.

In 1750 Voltaire, who had been coyly resisting Frederick's pressing invitations to join him at Potsdam, finally went. His departure was accelerated by two circumstances, first, the complete indifference of Louis XV, who refused to realise that France was about to suffer an irreparable loss by Arouet's secession, and secondly, the disquieting admiration expressed by Frederick for Baculard d'Arnaud whom he pretended to regard as the rising sun. Voltaire's amour-propre was not proof against this double assault. Meanwhile Malesherbes had shouldered a heavy responsibility by taking over control of the censorship. Essentially fair-minded, though secretly in sympathy with the anti-traditional movement, he reinstated Fréron, who at this time had regularised his domestic situation by wedding his niece by marriage, with whom he had been living for some years. Completely informed through correspondents as to Voltaire's antics in Germany, which were beginning to annoy Frederick, he learned that Arouet, at a dinner-party and in the presence of the Crown Prince and several French guests, had maliciously pretended to have received news that Fréron had been sent to the galleys. Also, Thieriot, Voltaire's correspondent in Paris, showed Fréron a letter from Berlin which clearly indicated that Voltaire was determined to ruin him. "Sooner or later," it ran, "Fréron will get what happened to Baculard d'Arnaud. He will be hunted out, if not worse, and perhaps, Prussian as I am, I'll find the secret for silencing this dog." His representations to Malesherbes proving useless, Fréron slipped into a review of the memoirs of Ninon de Lenclos, a discreet but recognisable and damning sketch of Arouet's moral character. "Sublime in some of his writings, base in all his actions; sometimes happy in his depiction of great passions, always occupied with petty ones . . . changing his dogma according to time and place; an independent in London, a Catholic in Paris, a pious

humbug in Austria, a tolerant in Germany. . . ."
Such are a few of the details which compose this
terrible indictment. Voltaire, in one of his classic
outbursts of hysterical rage, ordered his niece to
raise the hue and cry, which she did, much to the
amusement of Parisian society. Malesherbes weakly
allowed himself to be employed as the instrument
of Voltaire's revenge and the *Lettres* were again suppressed. Fréron was not, however, without friends.
Stanislas, the ex-King of Poland and father-in-law of
Louis XV, was an ardent Catholic. He had long
admired Fréron's defence of the traditional elements
in French literature and social life, and it was thanks
to his urgent personal appeal to Malesherbes that the
critic was allowed, in 1752, to resume his functions.
It is interesting to observe that Voltaire also wrote
on behalf of his enemy—an act of prudence rather
than of generosity, since it was due to the pressure
of his French colleagues in Berlin. Probably Fréron
had a bad quarter of an hour with the head of the
censorship, for it was some time before he again
succumbed to his "secret itch." In November 1752,
an incident occurred which served to show him that
he was closely watched. Commenting on Dubourg's
translation of Bolingbroke's *Letters on the Study of
History*, Fréron drew attention to the impropriety of
Bolingbroke's conduct, whilst a guest of Louis XIV,
in identifying himself with the opinions of the French
libertins who were active in sapping the authority of the State religion and government. To the
astonishment of even the inspector of the censorship,

d'Hémery, the *Lettres sur quelques Écrits* were suppressed. Bolingbroke had left a strong clique of
supporters, not the least important of whom was
Voltaire, though of course his direct participation in
this act of intolerance cannot be proved as he was
still in Germany. The *Lettres* were resumed after a
few weeks, but Fréron learned another lesson in
prudence.

The friendship of Stanislas, who called him to Versailles to present him to the Queen, was an infinite
consolation to the harassed editor for, like many
intelligent men at this time, he realised with sinking
heart that the old order was the object of a carefully
planned attack organised by a powerful group of
intellectuals who had sworn to annihilate the authority of the Church by substituting for a religion based
on faith a so-called religion, Deism, founded as they
averred on nature, reason, and humanity. In place
of the old morality which had its roots in obedience
to the will of God as interpreted by the priests of
the Catholic Church, these intellectuals, or *philosophes*
as they dubbed themselves, advocated a lay morality.
"Virtue," said Toussaint in 1748 in his popular *Des
mœurs*, "is a constant fidelity in fulfilling the obligations dictated to us by our reason." The idea was
by no means a new one. Bayle had already discussed the possibility of the compatibility of atheism
and morality. Diderot, Voltaire, Montesquieu, and
a dozen others advocated "natural" morality. Duclos,
though fully alive to the necessity for political and
economic reform, and in many respects a confirmed

journalist was under no illusion as to the political consequences of wholesale impiety. He realised that the spirit of revolt against orthodoxy in religion was almost inevitably bound to extend to government.

In 1751 was founded the *Encyclopédie*, the Bible of the *philosophes*. This vast compilation, edited by Diderot and d'Alembert, was a detailed survey of every branch of contemporary knowledge, but its real importance lay in its interpretative method which was rationalistic. It was an insidious and systematic attack levelled at the traditional authority of the Church, and it can readily be seen how easy it was to insert destructive propaganda in out-of-the-way corners of this huge edifice. The plan was ingeniously simple and consisted in writing perfectly orthodox articles under the rubrics likely to attract the attention of the censors who innocently passed over unpromising contributions on technical and dry-looking subjects which concealed, however, audacious and reactionary opinions. Diderot's was the dynamic force which energised the *Encyclopédie*. D'Alembert, constitutionally timid and easily irritated, was the wrong type of man to control an enterprise of this sort, which from the first was an object of suspicion to the authorities. The articles on religious subjects disgusted Voltaire by their tameness and he contributed very little to the work. Besides, Arouet found it difficult to acquire any great enthusiasm for a publication in which he was a mere contributor and not, as ordinarily, the directive mind. However, the general aims of the *Encyclopédie* being identical with his own, he encouraged the editors in their efforts to "crush the infamous one," as he called the Catholic Church in that well-known phrase which occurs in so many of his letters at this period— *Écrasez l'infâme!* But possibly the chief cause of Voltaire's lukewarmness was this. More passionate than his brother *philosophes*—excepting always Diderot— he realised that the effect of the Encyclopædist propaganda must be slow in making itself felt. Almost four thousand subscribers had been enrolled, but the cost of the work limited its sale to the wealthy possessors of private libraries who were already converted to the new ideas. Barbier, the Paris advocate, whose voluminous *Journal* is usually considered as a fair reflection of middle-class opinion, tells us definitely that the *Encyclopédie* was not well known to the bourgeoisie, whilst its great size made it impossible as a work to be passed from hand to hand amongst the people and the lower middle classes who were, however, eagerly curious about literature of this sort. That is why Arouet later produced his *Dictionnaire philosophique*, a portable, miniature *Encyclopédie*, but written in a scintillating, attractive style and with deadly lucidity.

The *Encyclopédie*, however, received an excellent send-off. Mme de Pompadour set the fashion by protecting it and the Court purchased it. But Diderot, whose *Pensées philosophiques* had been condemned by the Parlement in 1746, was a suspected atheist. In 1752, a priest, who like many of his brethren had espoused the new opinions, submitted a thesis to the Sorbonne where, owing to carelessness on the part of a censor, it was accepted, but later condemned as scandalously unorthodox. Now, it was known that the work in question was inspired, if not written, by Diderot. The Church, suddenly alive to the insidious propaganda emanating from the *Encyclopédie*, demanded and obtained its suppression, but the head of the censorship, Malesherbes, himself frustrated the searches of his own police by lending his own residence as a hiding-place for the plates of the prohibited volumes. Owing to the influence of the King's mistress the *Encyclopédie*, although not exposed publicly for sale, continued to appear, but its suppression frightened the timid d'Alembert and he lived in a constant state of panic, to the amusement of the gallant Voltaire who, from the security of Switzerland, bravely exhorted his nervous colleague to carry on the good work.

The publication of the *Encyclopédie* threw into relief the order of battle of the two opposing factions. On the one hand were the Encyclopædists or *philosophes*, as they loved to call themselves, generalled by Voltaire; on the other stood the anti-Encyclopædists or *anti-philosophes*, fighting a losing battle for tradition against the onslaught of rationalism. The army of the *philosophes* presented many shades of opinion, and some of its most eminent members like Montesquieu, Buffon, and Voltaire had very little part in the *Encyclopédie*, the most active contributor to which was a third-rate writer, the chevalier de Jaucourt, who was, however, ably seconded by

Parlement, who suspended their hereditary feud to attack a common foe. The Court was divided because Louis XV, much as he detested the new ideas, evinced the most complete apathy regarding their progress. The Queen, the Dauphin, and Stanislas warmly supported the Church, whilst Pompadour, perturbed as to her post-mortem situation and angered against the Jesuits, who refused her absolution on her own conditions, naturally supported the Encyclopædists because they were anti-clerical. Unfortunately for the *anti-philosophes*, their party, with the exception of Fréron, included practically no men of eminence in the field of letters. Boyer, the Bishop of Mirepoix, "the ass of Mirepoix," as Voltaire facetiously called him, was more pious than stimulating, and his death in 1755 made little difference to the cause of the traditionalists. The Catholics had one powerful weapon, a financial one, which they used to pierce the scaly armour of royal indifference. In 1757, for example, when assessing the amount of its "gratuitous gifts" or annual contribution to the royal exchequer, the Church, through its general assemblies, urgently represented to Louis the danger of tolerating the propaganda of the *philosophes*. The King, who was busy playing off the clericals against the Parlement, made promises and pocketed the money, but the *Encyclopédie* continued to appear. Fréron attacked it untiringly in his new paper, *L'Année littéraire*, but realised the fundamental weakness of his colleagues. "The apologist of religion," he wrote, "should possess the great art of interesting his readers. He should know how to temper the aridity of theological argument by the graces of style and should add to his erudition the qualities of the *littérateur* and the man of taste." He himself undoubtedly possessed these talents, which he continued to exercise with caution at the expense of Voltaire and his colleagues. In 1758, he boldly denounced the *Encyclopédie* as a scandalous work. D'Alembert, as usual, invoked the protection of Malesherbes and demanded the punishment of Fréron, but Malesherbes firmly refused to interfere with the liberty of criticism. Thus encouraged, Fréron maliciously reviewed an *anti-philosophe* book called *L'Histoire des Cacouacs*, and amused himself hugely. D'Alembert again complained and, in reply to a letter from Malesherbes, Fréron exposed his position. After citing some of the passages in the *Encyclopédie* in which he had been personally attacked, he added: "I am ignorant of the art of subterranean intrigue and base manœuvres. I have no other ambition but to work as a man of letters recognised by the Government; to live as a good citizen and to bring up my family properly. I respect in my conduct as in my writings, religion, morality, the State, and my superiors." The *philosophes* had already tried to deprive Fréron of the protection of Stanislas through the latter's minister, the comte de Tressan, who depended upon them to obtain election to the Academy. De Tressan made himself the tool of the *philosophes* and attempted to compromise the journalist in the eyes of his royal protector, who peremptorily

gentlemen; I do not envy their talents because I think I possess as many as they attribute to themselves. Nor do I covet their fortune which I can manage to do without, nor their literary honours which are only flattering when deserved, nor the consideration that they enjoy which is extremely equivocal." D'Alembert was finally routed in 1758, when Fréron, in a criticism of his translation of the *Annals* of Tacitus, wickedly showed up the limitations of his classical scholarship. D'Alembert ran squealing to Malesherbes, who told him bluntly that he would not interfere, so the disappointed mathematician retired from the *Encyclopédie*. In the following year the grave scandal provoked by the appearance of an atheistic work by Helvétius, a member of the "philosophic" group though not a contributor to the *Encyclopédie*, brought matters to a head and the privilege to print that work was withdrawn.

During this time Fréron had continued, in the *Année littéraire*, to lend his support to *anti-philosophes* like Moreau and his friend Palissot. He pretended to admire Voltaire, though the latter, like his colleagues, was fully alive to the innuendo concealed in Fréron's eulogies. The battle had now reached a critical stage and Voltaire, smarting under the just but merciless review of his play, *La Femme qui a raison*, in which he was compared to Lesage's immortal Archbishop of Granada, secretly began a work that was to make Fréron the laughing-stock of Europe. But otherwise he had not been idle.

His satiric poem, *Le Pauvre Diable*, published in 1758, justifies the verdict of the abbé Trublet, who shared with Fréron the honour of being vilified in it. "A fool could have written those verses but he would not have let them stand." The poem is a depressing suite of personal and abusive epithets, descending sometimes to language so foul as to be unprintable. Fréron is reviled as a tatterdemalion who keeps body and soul together by besmirching the reputations of estimable writers, a puddler in the "sewers of Helicon," a criminal in the world of literature, branded on the omoplate with the fleur-de-lis of public contempt, a cowardly Zoilus, a defrocked priest. But why enumerate all the items in this sorry catalogue of puerilities which is interesting merely as evidence of the disintegrating influence exercised by Fréron's criticism on a man who gloried in the title of *arbiter elegantiarum* in matters of literary taste? Scratch a Voltaire and you find a guttersnipe!

The campaign of 1760 opened inauspiciously for the *philosophes*. A poet of some merit and an ardent Churchman, Lefranc de Pompignan, chose the moment of his election to the *Académie française* to deliver a veiled but obvious attack on the enemies of the Church and State at a full session of the Immortals. This was literally carrying the war into the hostile camp, for the Academy was by this time practically a preserve of the intellectuals. Lefranc de Pompignan has been rightly blamed for this improper departure from established procedure, which can only be justified by the exigency of the situation. In

dignified but telling phrases he scarified the anti-
religious propaganda of the free-thinkers whom he
accused of "sapping the foundations of the altar and
the throne." Voltaire, though his name was not, of
course, mentioned, had no difficulty in identifying
himself as the author chiefly responsible for the "succession of scandalous libels, insolent verses, frivolous
and licentious writings" condemned by the speaker.
Rushing to the attack, he bombarded Lefranc with
the pitiless hail of his "Quand," "Car," "Ah! ah!"
"Pour," "Qui," "Quoi," mercifully administering the
coup de grâce to his reeling victim with *La Vanité*,
a poem in the best Voltairian manner.

In May of 1760, Palissot produced at the *Comédie
française* his satire *Les Philosophes*, in which Diderot,
Helvétius, Rousseau, Duclos, Mme Geoffrin the
salonnière, and Mlle Clairon the actress were exposed to ridicule. The audience roared with laughter
to see Crispin (Rousseau), the natural man, appear
on the stage on all fours munching a lettuce. Palissot,
backed by the princesse de Robecq and the duc de
Choiseul, snapped his fingers at the censorship. The
philosophes, beside themselves with rage, turned to
their chief for help, but Voltaire, who was not attacked
in the play and who moreover was secretly in correspondence with the author, appeased his colleagues
by pretending to withdraw his *Médime* from the
Comédie française. With typical perfidy, he wrote
at this time to d'Argental:

I therefore implore Mlle Clairon to say that I have withdrawn *Médime*; she will play it afterwards when she likes,

but I want to seem indignant at the play of the *Frogs* against the *Socrates* (*philosophes*).   I am much more annoyed at the reply, entitled *La Vision*, in which Mme de Robecq, who is on her deathbed, is insulted.   It is the most mortal blow which the *philosophes* could inflict on themselves.

As a commentary on Voltaire's state of mind this letter is invaluable.   The larger issue had temporarily faded from his thoughts.   Wholly engrossed now in his projected attack on Fréron, he was concentrating all his energy on this personal quarrel.   The overtures to Palissot reveal one aspect of his plan, which was to expose Fréron to the ridicule of Europe, to isolate him from his friends, and finally to silence him for ever by getting rid of the *Année littéraire*. If his colleagues could be used to further this scheme he would use them.   If not, as in the case of Palissot's play, he could amuse them with promises and a specious show of friendship.   Early in June Voltaire's eagerly awaited and much advertised comedy *L'Écossaise* was published.   This was to be the death-blow to Fréron's reputation and, incidentally, a warning to all meddling journalists to keep their pens off the sacrosanct productions of the *philosophes*.

Arouet, who was much more dramatic off the stage than on it, excelled himself in the subterfuges which he adopted to cover up his tracks.   The *Écossaise* was given out as the work of a Scottish Presbyterian minister, translated into French by a certain Jérôme Carré.   Meanwhile word was passed from Switzerland to the clique to get ready for the first per-

formance on 29 July.   Fréron gave the comedy a
long notice on 3 June.

The gazetteer who plays a *postiche* rôle in the *Écossaise* is
called Frelon [he wrote].   He is qualified as a pamphleteer,
a rogue, a toad, a lizard, an adder, a spider, a viper's tongue,
a crack-brained fellow, a soul of mud, a lackey, an impudent
cowardly scamp, a spy, a dog, etc.   I hear that some petty
ink-slingers claim that I am the person designated under the
name of Frelon.   All right; let them believe it or pretend to
believe it.   Let them try even to make others believe it.
But if it is really me that the author is aiming at, I conclude
from that very fact that it is not M. de Voltaire who wrote
this play.   That eminent poet who possesses a great deal of
genius, especially the genius of invention, would not have
stooped to plagiarise M. Piron, who long before the *Écossaise*
very ingeniously called me Frelon; it is true that he himself
stole this charming idea, this incredibly witty effort, from
M. Chevrier, an infinitely funny writer.   Again, would M. de
Voltaire ever have dared to call me a *fripon*?   He knows
manners and he is too well aware of what he owes to himself
and to others.

The censor, feeling that Voltaire had gone too far, suggested that "Guêpe" (wasp) should be substituted for
"Frelon" (hornet), but the victim himself urbanely insisted upon the actors retaining the original title.   He
pluckily attended the first performance with his wife
and had the moral courage to sit through the derisive
laughter which greeted every appearance of Frelon
on the stage.   Voltaire's cabal, led by the Teuton,
Grimm, and aided by Diderot and Marmontel—
Duclos and d'Alembert excused themselves—secured

a run of sixteen performances, which in those days
was very considerable, and Voltaire further excited
the public against his victim in a *Requête aux Parisiens*,
issued on the eve of the play. Some of the more
decent-minded of the *philosophes* felt that Arouet
had sacrificed his dignity and something of his reputation as a dramatic author, for the *Écossaise* had
purely a *succès de scandale*: as a literary production
it was without merit. The only person who emerged
from this affair with any credit was Fréron himself,
who went straight from the theatre to his study and
penned a facetious account of what he called "La
grande Bataille."

This narrative is much more amusing than the
comedy itself. An extract will serve to indicate the
timbre of the article:

The redoubtable Dortidius (Diderot) was in the centre of
the army: he had been unanimously elected generalissimo.
His countenance was inflamed, his glances furious, his hair
dishevelled, all his senses agitated as, when possessed by his
divine enthusiasm, he pronounces his oracles on the philosophic tripod. This centre included the flower of the troops,
i.e. all those who are working at that great dictionary "whose
suspension makes Europe groan,"[1] the typographers who
printed it, the booksellers who retail it, and their shopboys.

Fréron maliciously went on to picture the more
prudent of Voltaire's friends, like Hénault and the
comte d'Argental, waiting in the Tuileries for news
of the engagement, the growing enthusiasm with
which they greeted the reported success of each *bon*

[1] An expression used by the *philosophes*.

mot and the grand *Te Voltairium* celebrating the final victory.

Arouet, realising that his *coup* had missed, asked Thieriot to collect every available scrap of information about Fréron's life, and these he worked up into a series of scurrilous *Anecdotes*, published, as usual, anonymously. The journalist retorted with his famous *Portrait de Sadi*, which purported to be the biography of a Persian poet of the thirteenth century, though of course everyone recognised that Sadi was Voltaire. He wrote:

Sadi shamelessly copied every author who fell into his hands: the Bedouin Arabs do not pillage caravans with more audacity. After enriching himself with thefts and plagiarisms, he ended like Plautus's miser who surprised his left hand robbing his right. He pillaged himself. We possess more than twenty volumes of Sadi and there is not one which offers a new idea; he had imagination only in expression. In other words, with him form was everything and content did not exist. . . . He has written numerous verses but has never been a poet. People will take good care not to inscribe him among the historians, since truth, the primary characteristic of the historian, is not to be found in Sadi. . . . What name shall we give him then? That of philosopher? Sadi a philosopher! Anyone who had called him that would have been hooted at derisively. *Bel esprit* and then what? *Bel esprit*. Such is the title which Persians (Frenchmen) accord to Sadi. . . . He has smeared over his works a varnish of morality and humanity which favourably disposes the reader towards him. One would be tempted to believe that his was the most sublime and sympathetic soul, the soul of a demi-god. Yet all the histories of his time represent him in a very different light. It is said that in his conduct he was merely a man and a very little man, affecting in his books contempt of fame, of grandeur, and of fortune; in his private life a base courtier, avid of the most ephemeral glory and moreover possessed by the demon of riches, at every moment eulogising friendship yet unable to deserve or to keep a friend. The vulture of envy gnawed at his heart; jealousy infected him with her most venomous poisons. . . . He sickened with grief at the sight of the busts of Homer and Virgil. He ardently wished that a second deluge might inundate the globe so that his works alone should survive to attest to a new world that Sadi was the only genius who shone in the old one. He moved only through the tortuous paths of intrigue: he clumsily employed the grossest methods to slake his burning thirst for glory and for wealth or to immolate to his vengeance anyone who did not prostrate himself before his merit. He despised the great yet there was no baseness, no trick which he did not employ to live in their intimacy. . . .

Not one of Voltaire's vices but finds its niche in this dreadful mosaic.

It was especially in literary quarrels that he afforded the world the spectacle of puerile outbursts of temper and petulance. Then he was like a drunken man abandoning himself to all the caprices of a disordered brain. . . . I will not speak of his avarice. Armenians and Jews he prosecuted in lawsuits which covered him with obloquy. Every month he issued a new edition which he disowned the month following. He sold wine and wheat as he sold verses. The cleverest Hebrews confessed that they could not calculate like him, and they regarded him with the respect of disciples for a master. His vanity was intolerable, at once revolting to common sense and to humanity. He raised this vice to the

point of folly, nay, of fury.   The monstrous pride of Caligula
was naught in comparison to the pride of Sadi.   The most
moderate criticism appeared to him a crime worthy of death,
and yet it was to criticism alone that he owed the few real
beauties which are sometimes found in his works.

We can only conjecture what was the effect of the
Portrait de Sadi on Voltaire, who dared not, of course,
take notice of it.   "Jean Fréron" or "Maître Ali-
boron," to cite the commonest of the nicknames
humorously applied to the journalist by Arouet,
had now acquired considerable skill in the art of
satirising his enemies without running foul of the censorship.   His literary criticisms were sound, moderate,
and fair, and even his censors, who sometimes favoured
the philosophic party, were rarely able to find fault
with them.   Besides, he was now something of a
personage.   Protected by Stanislas and Queen Marie
Leczinska, a member of three provincial academies,
esteemed and feared for the justice and ruthlessness
of his critical pronouncements, he had succeeded,
moreover, in awakening in Malesherbes the uneasy
feeling that his conduct in regard to the editor of
the *Année littéraire* had not always been above
reproach.

In 1760, Voltaire, amid much publicity, adopted a
grand-niece of Thomas Corneille, brother of the great
tragedian.   It was Fréron who first drew public
attention to the plight of this girl and her father,
for whom he arranged a benefit performance at the
Comédie française.   To Voltaire's fury, the following
ambiguous comment appeared in the *Année littéraire*,

striking a discordant note in the general pæan of admiration:

> You cannot imagine the fuss which M. de Voltaire's generosity is making in society. It has been referred to in the gazettes, in the journals, and in all the public papers, and I am persuaded that these pompous announcements are causing great pain to this modest poet who knows that the chief merit of praiseworthy acts is the secrecy which attaches to them. . . . It must be admitted that on leaving the convent Mlle Corneille is going to fall into good hands.

It is true that the concluding observation is cruel and malicious: whether it was merited depends on one's estimate of Voltaire's character and his qualifications for the rôle of *éducateur de jeunesse*. In any case the barb sank home. Every influence was exerted to have Fréron punished. Mlle Corneille was urged to prosecute the journalist who had published some accurate facts concerning her father who was a thoroughly worthless individual. For Voltaire, and he was a connoisseur in such matters, the only adequate punishment for Fréron was "a horse-whipping." He devoted a stanza to him in his *Pucelle* in which Fréron appeared as a galley slave. A more successful effort was the famous epigram:

> L'autre jour au fond d'un vallon
> Un serpent piqua Jean Fréron.
> Que pensez-vous qu'il arriva?
> Ce fut le serpent qui creva.

Fréron retaliated by quoting the original, written a hundred years before, and pointed out that the canto in which he was vilified in the *Pucelle* was clumsily imitated from *Don Quixote*. At every turn, it seemed to Voltaire, his enemy lay in wait, and in the midst of his greatest victories he came to dread that ironical, suggestive phrase in the *Année littéraire*, darkening with its shadow the rosy flush of triumph. When, for example, after his rehabilitation of the unfortunate Protestant Calas, the victim of a judicial blunder, Voltaire, in the dual rôle of apostle of tolerance and avenger of injustice, was complacently basking in the sun of popular adulation it was Fréron who dared to suggest that the motives for Arouet's conduct were not those of an altruist and humanitarian but of an anti-clerical and a political malcontent.

Naturally enough, enthusiastic admirers of Voltaire have portrayed Fréron as the embodiment of intolerance and of dogmatic superstition and as hostile to any form of progress. Nothing is farther from the truth. In his private life he was far from being a *dévot* or an ascetic, though he was by no means the crapulous individual depicted by Arouet in the *Anecdotes*. He realised, as did Voltaire, that in the contemporary state of French society it was imperative that the people should have a religion if morality were to subsist at all. But where the *philosophes* would have substituted the worship of a "Supreme Being" for the old-established Christian faith, Fréron with his realistic mind saw that the reason of the common man was not sufficiently developed to grasp this metaphysical conception of a deity, and that, deprived of his foundation of inherited religious beliefs, he would inevitably—as he did—lapse into irreligion with grave consequences to the social equilibrium.

Fully aware of the intoxicating effects of rationalistic propaganda on the crude mentality of the masses, Fréron sounded a note of warning to young writers. "Everything which is harmful to religion and morality, however happily it is phrased, defiles, nay enfeebles, the reputation of a writer. Decent mediocrity is a thousand times to be preferred to cynical superiority." The iconoclastic tendencies of his age filled him with misgivings. "Nearly everyone mistakes his vocation. People with no conception of metaphysics write on the most impalpable matters; people with no principles of their own attack those which are already established; men of no genius compose dramatic and other poems whilst those with no taste write in genres where taste is most essential."

Like Voltaire, Fréron fought shy of metaphysical questions as being outside the scope of human reason. But where Voltaire dismissed such matters as those of free will and divine goodness as of no importance in life, the journalist with greater realism perceived that such problems lie at the very roots of existence and adopted the common-sense view that it is safer in such things to follow the promptings of our hearts than to adopt the sorry doctrine of the materialist. Whilst admitting that the *geometric mind* had accustomed the men of the new age to reflect on many fruitful subjects formerly considered as outside their domain, Fréron regretted the decay of true sentiment so sadly evidenced in the state of contemporary poetry. And, though no supporter of the Anglomaniacs, he recommended his colleagues to read the English poets "with discretion" as a corrective to their own cold, metaphysical manner. More tolerant than Voltaire, who was incapable of a generous and objective appreciation of the great classics, either French or foreign, Fréron cited the divergent beauties of Homer, Virgil, Tasso, Milton, and Racine to show that there is no royal road to Parnassus. More eclectic than his enemy, he could see a place even for the popular *poissard* genre of a Vadé, "low, if you like, in the disdainful eyes of a certain philosophic dignity, but very agreeable to contemplate, whatever our sensitives say." Better, he thought, even literature of this sort which springs from real life than "all those sublime productions, those huge and wonderful dictionaries which certain people admire between their yawns and which are scarcely even read once and will never be reprinted." It is odd to find Fréron and Diderot in agreement against Voltaire, but, like Diderot, the journalist was a warm supporter of the new type of play, the *drame*, which was to take the place of the now obsolescent neo-classic tragedy.

What has produced so many monotonous and mediocre dramas is this rule to which authors are restricted. They tell us because they have heard it said, that vice must be punished and virtue rewarded, that the theatre must purge the passions. This fine dictum has made their works cold, constrained, and improbable. What is the art and the object of the tragic scene? To please by touching the spectator and by communicating to his heart the passions which are represented on the stage. That is the secret of Melpomene.

Fréron saw that Voltaire's attempts to bring the theatre nearer to nature were superficial, since they were confined to such externals as costume and stage setting.

> Show us real Chinese [he admonished], not as in that mediocre tragedy the *Orphelin de la Chine*, a drama without colour or character. Let us see the Japanese, who for a single insulting phrase dies of rage and grief. Let the usages, the customs of each nation be employed skilfully: in a word, let the tragic writer transport us to the very place of the action. Let him never lose sight of nature, and then we shall have not only novel but new tragedies.

It is said that Voltaire, questioned once by a foreigner as to who was the soundest literary critic in France, directed his visitor to Fréron. If this is true it does him honour, though it would have been an act of simple justice. There is, alas! nothing in his conduct towards the journalist which permits us to believe this anecdote. The old "orang-outang of Ferney" became more vindictive with the passing years.

The battle between orthodoxy and rationalism still raged. The expulsion of the Jesuits in 1763, although a victory for the *philosophes*, was also one for the Parlement, as it was indeed for the Jansenists. Voltaire, whose principal weapon against Catholicism was history, suddenly found his authority questioned by scholars like Nonotte and Greffet, whilst his reputation as a poet was assailed by Clément, Gilbert, Imbert, and of course by Fréron. His unfortunate commentary on Corneille's *Cid*, in which his jealousy got the better of his discretion, produced a shocked surprise even amongst his disciples. Nonotte's *Erreurs de Voltaire* revealed him as an unscrupulous writer who did not hesitate to manufacture sources where none were available and to distort the facts of history to support a thesis. It became clear to many that in his zeal to destroy religious intolerance none was more fanatically intolerant than Arouet himself. Fréron wisely left the refutation of Voltaire's naïve blunders in theology and in ancient history to professionals. His relations with the censorship were becoming increasingly difficult and, indeed, inexplicable. Stanislas had died in 1766, followed shortly after by Queen Marie Leczinska, so that the journalist dared not risk an encounter with Malesherbes. For four years, from 1766 until 1770, he submitted to the humiliation of having critical articles returned to him with the simple intimation that the censor refused permission to print. This occurred only when the works of the *philosophes* were under review. The explanation of the mystery was divulged by Fréron to his readers in 1772. As a result of an arrangement agreed to by Fréron, the identity of the censor of the *Année littéraire* was to remain a secret to all save Malesherbes and an official who acted as intermediary between the editor and his censor who, as we now know, was a certain Coqueley de Chausse-

they have neither his wit, his reminiscences, his repertoire, nor the magic of his style, they can only mimic his audacity, his irreligion, his obscenities, the clash of his ideas, his verbal antitheses, his trick of associating incongruous or widely divergent subjects—in a word, all his defects. The courtiers of Alexander, aping their master, manage to copy perfectly only his stoop.

But the end of the conflict was in sight. Fréron, single-handed, knew that defeat was inevitable, but he fought gamely to the end. In 1774, the *Année littéraire* took Grimm and Diderot severely to task for their lack of patriotism in vilifying their own country when on a visit to the Court of Catherine of Russia, that fervent admirer of tolerance and humanitarianism—in the abstract. With a new Government in power which shared their ideas, the *philosophes* succeeded in getting the *Année littéraire* suspended for three months. In 1776, taking advantage of Fréron's illness, the Voltairians again besieged the authorities, and on 10 March the editor of the *Année littéraire* was informed that his privilege to print had been revoked. Undaunted, the old warrior sent his wife to plead with Louis XVI in person, and she rushed back from Versailles to Paris with the good news that her husband was reinstated. But Fréron was never to know it, for he was dead.

When the news of his death was published, Fréron's enemies preserved a decent silence. All save Voltaire, who had the inhuman cruelty to disseminate the lying tale that Mme Fréron had approached him for financial aid, begging him also to find a husband for her daughter as he had done for Mlle Corneille. "I replied," Voltaire reported himself as saying, "that if Fréron has written a *Cid*, a *Cinna*, or a *Polyeucte* I shall have no difficulty in getting her married."

In the *Dictionnaire philosophique* we find this estimable sentiment by Voltaire: "It is clear that anyone who persecutes his fellow-man because he is not of his opinion is a monster." What is not so clear is the precise epithet which the same author would have applied to Monsieur de Voltaire, comte de Tournay and Seigneur de Ferney, who stooped to strike at a dead man by smirching the reputation of a widow and her daughter. So great is the indulgence which posterity extends to genius that one hesitates to characterise such conduct, but with all possible deference to the talents of that great man, Monsieur de Voltaire behaved in this occurrence like an ordinary blackguard.

PLAYHOUSES

An August afternoon in Paris in the thirty-third year of the reign of Louis XV, once nicknamed by a pathetically optimistic nation Louis the Well-beloved. A westering sun beats white and hotly on the helmet dome of the *Palais de Mazarin* and lays a barrage of light on the river. Much beglassed carriages, rumbling along the Faubourg Saint-Germain, emerge from a flashing nimbus into the cool darkness of the narrow rue des Fossés-Saint-Germain and halt before the doors of the *Comédie française*. Arrogantly servile footmen in livery leap down, open doors and place steps in position for the descent of *madame la marquise*, who is gallantly handed down by her *sigisbée*, magnificent in mauve shot with silver and peering with fashionable, affected myopia at the loungers through his gold lorgnette. Inside the ancient House of Molière the three tiers of boxes are already full and an excited tumult arises from the parterre where, in the space of seven hundred square feet, are packed some hundreds of spectators, standing. All are men, for not even in this age of progress would a very woman of the town dare to enter this male sanctuary. The *premières loges* present the mass impression of a perfumed and gaily-coloured shimmering garden. Peruked and panniered ladies flash provocative glances over their fans at whispering cavaliers. Cynical dowagers converse loudly in dragging syllables and "at every word a reputation dies." In her stage box Mlle Clairon the actress, in full Court dress and her enormous wig arranged *en rhinocéros*, interrupts with peals of silvery laughter the exquisite little abbé who is relating a scandalous anecdote about the detested Mme de Pompadour—*la Poisson*, as they call her. In the orchestra seats and in front of the parterre there is a sprinkling of authors. Here is the gossipy Collé and here Saint-Foix, the comic author, talking to Marivaux, whose intelligent, restless eyes flicker over the house, observing and registering the eternal comedy of love and jealousy which is being enacted in the boxes. The graceless, fashionable novelist, Crébillon the younger, is the cynosure of a hundred feminine lorgnettes, a fact of which he is complacently aware as he jokes with a friend about his father's tragedy *Catilina* which has been twenty mortal years on the stocks. Now, it appears, the septuagenarian must finish it, for Pompadour, who is at daggers drawn with Voltaire, has taken the veteran tragic poet under her protection and, much to his embarrassment, insists on his entering the lists against his young and redoubtable rival. Collé takes snuff and leans back contentedly. This promises to be a great day for his diary. "I hear from the actors," he remarks, "that Arouet has distributed four hundred free parterre tickets amongst his friends. The new tragedy should be a success." For this is the first performance of Voltaire's *Sémiramis* and the *Comédiens du Roi* have gone to the expense of a new setting in honour of the occasion. Besides, it is rumoured that there is to be a ghost, an English idea picked up by Voltaire in London at the performance of some barbaric play by some outlandish person of whom nobody has ever heard. In the foyer a gaunt and sardonic man is explaining volubly and with much gesticulation to the Prince of Würtemberg that he cannot possibly come to Versailles for supper. "But surely, Monsieur de Voltaire, you sometimes go to see your King." "No, Prince, for he receives only at his *petit lever*. Can you imagine it? *That man* rises sometimes at ten, sometimes at noon, and often not till two in the afternoon. So, the last time I saw him I said: 'Sire, when your Majesty desires to see me I should be grateful if you would send me your commands.'" There is a little murmur of shocked protest from the bystanders at the words *cet homme* used in regard to the monarch, but the high-pitched, self-assured voice runs on with an under-quiver of suppressed venom belied by the mischievous eyes, for Voltaire is now telling the slightly bored princeling about the cabal of Crébillon's supporters which is at that moment in the theatre, and about the stupid blockheads who object to his title *Sémiramis* just because *père* Crébillon produced a tragedy of the same name twenty (or was it fifty?) years ago. "As if, *mon prince*," continues the eldritch voice—"as if, forsooth, these classical subjects were not common property." But now a *huissier* is at Voltaire's elbow and the thin legs twinkle off to the auditorium where, from the commanding heights of a *troisième loge*, the author will witness the progress of his play and keep an eye on his hirelings in the parterre.

The groundlings are noisy but good-humoured. A running fire of witticisms greets the arrival of a Court abbé who appears in one of the boxes squiring two well-known Parisian society beauties. Shouts of "Place aux dames!" "Haut les bras, monsieur l'abbé!" send waves of mirth through the parterre, to the bewilderment of the spectators in the boxes who cannot penetrate the psychology of the people, ever ready on such hilarious occasions to hoot with laughter at the most pointless observations. The little abbé in a fury shouts down to the imperturbable soldiers stationed round the auditorium, but his words are drowned in the general hurly-burly. The *canaille* now turns its attention to the lemonade woman who is having a violent argument with a customer. In another corner of the parterre a knot of shopboys and lawyers' clerks is receiving instructions from a rake-helly fellow with a certain air, though dissipation has left tell-tale marks on his once clear-cut, aristocratic features. This is Voltaire's *chef de cabale*, the chevalier de la Morlière, novelist, adventurer, and ex-officer, one of those innumerable provincial gentlemen who flock in swarms to Paris to sell their pen or sword to the highest bidder.

Half-past five. The *moucheur* crawls out to snuff the candles. The traditional three knocks produce

an expectant hush and the curtain rises revealing on
each side of the stage four rows of seats separated
from the stage itself by a gilded balcony. The pseudo-
Babylonian setting by the brothers Flooz excites a
hurricane of applause from Voltaire's supporters in
the amphitheatre and pit, mingled with cat-calls and
hisses from the Crébillonites. On the stage, Grand-
val, in the rôle of Ninus, is declaiming to Mlle
Dumesnil who has the part of Sémiramis. The
Alexandrines are chanted rather than spoken, the
actor's voice rattling along the syllables like a boy's
stick on railings, and regularly at the end of the line
there is an appreciable pause. Ninus, dressed like
an officer of Louis XV's Household Regiment, is pom-
pously extolling his soldierly virtues. The phrases,
les vertus d'un soldat, un soldat tel que moi, excite the
impatience of one of the cabal. "Well, for Heaven's
sake make him a sergeant then!" he exclaims, to the
exquisite delight of the house which rocks with
merriment. Voltaire, livid with fury, splutters to
Mme du Châtelet who places a restraining hand on
his arm. Dumesnil's bell-like voice restores calm
once more, but the tumult breaks forth anew when a
fat revenue farmer in a stage seat, enraged by some
quip addressed to him from the parterre, orders an
exempt to arrest the offender who by this time is
glaring accusingly at the man behind him. Soon,
however, the situation is saved by Arouet's mer-
cenaries whose shocked cries for silence awaken the
somnolent guards to a sense of duty. Mme du
Châtelet mischievously points out to the author that

some of his hirelings, though applauding faithfully, are yawning fearsomely the while. Voltaire says nothing but stares with cold displeasure. His bearing is that of an offended monarch. One expects at every moment to hear him say, "We are not amused."

During the whole course of the play, a knot of fifty young men about town, grouped at the back of the stage, keeps up an incessant chatter punctuated with shrill cackles of laughter. Dumesnil looks daggers, which amuses them mightily. But now comes the moment for the eagerly expected *coup de théâtre*—the entrance of the ghost of Ninus. The actor glides on, but finds his way blocked by two dandies who insolently ignore his obsequious request to be allowed to pass. He dodges to the right, only to find an enormous financier in his path. His agonised whispers reach the audience. Voltaire's face is like a devil's. His quick mind foresees the inevitable catastrophe. Nothing save a miracle can avert that witticism which even now is crystallising into words in the brain of one of the audience. It comes like a thunderbolt and — perfection of irony!—from one of his own cabal, a fellow with a Cyrano de Bergerac nose who, vaguely aware that the shade of Ninus is being illegally interfered with in the execution of his duty, with stentorian voice bellows out indignantly, "Eh, bien! messieurs. Place à l'ombre!" Pandemonium is unchained, drowning the stage thunder which accompanies Sémiramis's tirade. Everyone had expected an unusual *dénouement*, but an impish Fate has turned indifferent tragedy into Gargantuan farce.

The curtain falls and pickpockets steal softly towards the exit with their booty of watches and silk hand-kerchiefs while their unconscious victims are wiping the tears of mirth from their vermilion faces. Voltaire's box is empty and in the carriage which bears him off to Sceaux his mind is even now formulating a letter of protest to Berryer, Lieutenant-Général de Police. Meanwhile, across the road, in the Café de Procope, once the haunt of Molière and of Racine, the gleeful crowd of fifth-rate playwrights is celebrating the monumental discomfiture of their brilliant and hated rival. The tragedy over, the eternal human comedy resumes.

The object of this impression is to indicate very generally the handicaps imposed by a system whereby not only did the Government, through its censorship, dictate the nature of the ideas which were to be expressed by the playwright, but actually, though in a more discreet fashion, so controlled the stage as to check the natural evolution of dramatic art in general. This aspect of the struggle between reaction, or progress, and tradition is so important that no account of eighteenth-century French life and ideas can be complete which neglects the history of the Parisian stage.

At the close of the seventeenth century Paris, with a population of eight hundred thousand, had three legitimate stages—the *Comédie française* or *Théâtre français*, the *Comédie italienne*, and the *Académie Royale de musique*, usually known as the *Opéra*. The *Comédie française*, as the eighteenth century knew it,

really originated in 1680 when Louis XIV, in a *lettre
de cachet* to the Lieutenant-General de Police, merged
two troupes of actors, those of the Hôtel de Bourgogne and those of the rue Guénégaud, into one
company, to be known henceforth as the King's
Players (*Les Comédiens du Roi*). The new troupe
was granted the exclusive right to produce stage
plays in Paris and its suburbs and received an annual
grant of twelve thousand francs from the Privy Purse
in 1682.   The actors constituted themselves into a
business company and established a pension scheme
whereby members of the cast who had purchased a
share drew an annuity of one thousand francs on
retirement, that is, usually after twenty years' service.   Various changes in the financial arrangements
were made throughout the eighteenth century, particularly in 1758, when the business affairs of the
Comédie française were reorganised by the State
Council without, however, substantially altering the
original system.

One of the first acts of the newly formed troupe
was to build a new theatre, which was erected in the
rue des Fossés-Saint-Germa.   to-day known as the
rue de l'Ancienne-Comédie.   This theatre, which was
opened in 1681 and was destined to endure until the
Revolution, was in the shape of a rectangle rounded at
one end. The other, occupied by the actors, was about
twelve metres wide, though the presence of three rows
of seats on the stage reduced its actual width to about
eight metres, whilst, as has been seen, the presence of
some fifty spectators at the back of the stage further

limited the space at the disposal of the producer.
Three rows of boxes enclosed the auditorium and
accommodated about four hundred spectators. Some
of these, the so-called *balcons*, overlooked the stage
on both sides and were directly above the stage seats.
Between the *balcons* and the boxes in the auditorium
were the two royal boxes, rounded in front and over-
hanging the orchestra which had much the appearance
of our modern "trench" arrangement, except that
the eighteenth-century musicians were hemmed in
by spectators whose proximity must have been as
irritating to the instrumentalists as the noise of the
music was to the playgoer. The parterre occupied
an area of 850 square feet (French) in the centre of
the theatre and held about six hundred people when
crowded. At the back of the parterre was the
amphitheatre which seated ninety persons who were
overlooked by the boxes at the back of the auditorium, whose occupants were thus situated about
twenty metres from the stage.

A more impracticable theatre it would scarcely be
possible to imagine, and it is interesting to note that
for one hundred years, whilst in Italy and even in
French provincial towns like Lyons the modern semi-
circular form of auditorium had been long in vogue,
the *Comédie française* clung obstinately to the incon-
venient rectangular hall, a relic of the days of Molière,
when the troupe had to play in a disused tennis-court.
For the rectangular form, whilst doubtless excellent
for battledore and shuttlecock, was impossible from
the point of view of the playgoer. The acoustics of

the eighteenth-century Parisian theatre were so bad that the actor had to strain his voice to reach the audience in the farthest boxes, so that the occupants of the *loges royales* were unpleasantly affected by the sight of his contortions and by the sound of his respiratory efforts. The people in the *balcons* or wing boxes never obtained a front view of the players, whilst those who were in the boxes directly facing the actors had to stand up in order to see on account of the pillars separating the boxes. Those in the lateral boxes were constrained to sit diagonally or to lean forward, and even then they never saw more than half the stage.

However, the greatest obstacle to theatrical illusion was the presence of spectators upon the stage itself, a practice common to the three Parisian theatres and also a relic of the old days when tennis-courts were used as playhouses and the auditorium was not large enough to accommodate all the spectators. This absurd custom is condemned by every eighteenth-century playwright and its persistence must be attributed to the avarice of the actors themselves who, though the chief sufferers, preferred to pocket their pride along with the extra receipts thus obtained rather than clear the stage. An eighteenth-century stage during the performance of a Racinian play was like a fashionable race-meeting minus the horses. Numbers of gaily dressed men about town, followed by their lackeys, gossiped and strolled about, crossing the stage to greet old friends, bowing to acquaintances in the boxes, and clattered off when

the whim seized them, for if you left before the end
of the first act your money was returned. A con-
tinual vendetta existed between the groundlings and
the audience on the stage, and it was quite common
for some choleric officer, apostrophised by a member
of the parterre, to step forward in front of the actor
and demand satisfaction in no uncertain voice. Often
before the play began young noblemen would stand
insolently gazing down at the *canaille*, ignoring the
appeals of the *orateur* or publicity manager who was
trying to announce the programme for the following
performance. Sometimes, as at the production of
Athalie, on 16 December, 1739, the curtain had to be
lowered before the end of the play on account of the
uproar on the stage. Incidents such as that which
occurred during Voltaire's *Sémiramis* were very frequent. A messenger, striving to bring a letter to the
King and fighting his way through a serried mass of
young bloods, was greeted with delighted shouts of
Place au facteur! at the production of the tragedy
of *Childeric*. Both at the *Comédie française* and at
the *Opéra* it was of course impossible to heighten the
dramatic illusion by the help of scenic effects, though
at the latter theatre in particular the decorator put
up a bold struggle against heavy odds. It was fortunate indeed that the unity of place existed as a
dramatic convention, and there is no doubt that it
was largely the presence of spectators on the stage
which prevented the abolition of this, the least
necessary of the three unities. Much of the senseless
criticism of French eighteenth-century tragedy by

foreigners is due to ignorance of prevailing stage conditions. Imagine Macbeth and Macduff "laying on" lustily, surrounded by grinning officers back on leave from the Flanders front, or Lady Macbeth in the sleep-walking scene groping her way on to the stage, or the gravediggers' scene from *Hamlet*! No, all dramatic art rests on convention and illusion, and if these are absent not even the genius of a Shakespeare can impress an audience.

Thanks to the generosity of a certain M. de Lauraguais, who gave the actors twelve thousand francs, the stage seats were removed from the *Comédie française* during the Easter recess of 1759. Part of the parterre was provided with seating to accommodate one hundred and eighty persons, and the amphitheatre was reduced to compensate for the space taken from the parterre to make the new section, which was called the *parquet*. Squeals arose, of course, from the little dandies, who held indignation meetings at the Café de Procope, but the reform was maintained and for the first time, on 23 April, 1759, the *Comédiens du Roi* played on a clear stage. A new era was thus inaugurated in the history of French drama. Authors were able to take full advantage of the arts of the costumier and scenic artist, whilst the old masterpieces of the seventeenth century obtained a new lease of life, now that the tragic grandeur of Racine and Corneille could be interpreted in a fitting *milieu*. Collé, the playwright, notes in his Diary:

One hears better and the illusion is greater. No longer does one see Cæsar brushing the dust from the wig of some fool seated in the front row of the stage seats and Mithridates expiring in the midst of one's aquaintances; the shade of Ninus jostling and elbowing a tax-farmer and Camille falling dead in the wings on top of Marivaux or Saint-Foix, who advance or retire, lending their aid to the murder of this Roman lady at the hands of her brother Horace, who spatters these two comic authors with her blood.

The necessary alterations cost twenty thousand francs, and it appears that the actors were not too pleased with their bargain. However, they were accorded permission to place seats on the stage for benefit performances (*pièces de capitation*). The stage of the *Comédie Italienne* was not cleared until 1761 and the *Opéra* soon followed suit.

Owing to the inferior status of the actor and the hierarchic composition of society, it was more difficult to obtain order in the auditorium itself. Here Molière had used his prestige to get Louis XIV to abolish the custom whereby members of the King's household troops were admitted to the theatre without paying. The result was a serious riot in which the theatre porter was massacred and the actors themselves almost murdered. Molière's complaint to Louis produced a royal decree providing for heavy penalties in case of a repetition of such scandals and exemplary punishment was meted out to the immediate offenders. It is clear, however, that these regulations were disobeyed, for in 1769 a royal ordinance was issued forbidding even officers of the royal household to enter the theatre without paying. The pages and lackeys of princely houses, who seem to have been

most obstreperous, were warned against interrupting
the play and were not allowed to occupy any seat
save in the parterre.   The ordinance forbade

those who are present at these performances, and particularly
those who are in the parterre, to commit any breach of the
peace either on entering or on leaving, to shout or make a
noise before the play begins and during the *entr'actes*, to
whistle, make cat-calls, to keep their hats on their heads,
or to interrupt the actors during the performance in any
way and under any pretext whatsoever.

Servants in livery were refused admittance to the
three State theatres even if they paid.   In 1751,
the *archers à robe courte*, who had hitherto policed
the audience, were replaced by regular troops, to the
great disgust of habitual playgoers like Collé, who
observes:

This produces great tranquillity but casts a certain gloom
over the theatre which makes me fear sometimes that I am
in some foreign country.   I miss our old French gaiety; the
parterre has a German look nowadays.   These French guards
are too pedantic in their method of controlling a lively nation
like ours, and then, I don't know, but all this business has
an air of servitude and slavery and I don't like being annoyed
like this in a public place of amusement.   Everything here
has a nasty air of despotism even in the smallest things.   We
are no longer allowed to feel that we are men.

It is rather odd to hear a playwright express these
views, but Collé was a strong traditionalist and by
temperament a confirmed grumbler.   Still, he echoes
the opinions of the man in the street, who was being

by third-rate authors who waived their rights to a royalty in their eagerness to be hissed by the justly indignant audience. The proof of this can be seen in the fact that on the rare occasions when the *Comédie française* went to special expense to stage or dress a good piece the house was always filled. There were other reasons connected with the internal administration of these theatres and the status of the actor which will emerge in the following pages. After all, the prices were far from exorbitant even when one makes allowance for the greater spending power of the franc or *livre* in the eighteenth century. The parterre cost twenty sous, the *troisièmes loges* thirty sous, the *deuxièmes loges* two francs, and all other seats four francs. These prices were, however, increased fifty per cent for the performance of new plays, though in a century notorious for its extravagance this would not deter even the lower middle classes from frequenting the theatre if they wanted to. Was Rousseau, who is usually careful of his facts, carried away by his prejudice against the stage to the point of misrepresenting the actual situation of the Parisian theatre? I do not think so. The *Lettre à d'Alembert sur les Spectacles* appeared in 1758, and in 1755 both the *Opéra* and the *Comédie française* were in grave financial difficulties, the actors of the latter house having borrowed over four hundred thousand francs in twelve years. In 1749, the *Opéra*, after having plunged a succession of directors into bankruptcy, was placed under municipal control. The free list was cut down and the theatre re-decorated in green

power. In 1716, Riccoboni's troupe came to Paris and was granted permission to call itself *Les Comédiens de Son Altesse Royale, Monsieur le duc d'Orléans*. After the death of the Regent they were known as *Les Comédiens italiens du Roi*.

Now, during the nineteen years' absence of these players the fairs of Saint-Laurent and of Saint-Germain, quick to step into the breach formed by the withdrawal of this popular theatre, put on imitations and fragments of the *comédies de genre* specially affected by the Italians. Parfait, a contemporary historian of the theatre, says that in 1706 at the Foire Saint-Germain there were no fewer than seven theatres offering "farces and comedies, half Italian and half French, interspersed with dances and intermezzos." A new type of play evolved, somewhat resembling a cross between our musical comedy and revue, in which current and contemporary plays were parodied to the huge delight of an audience drawn from all classes. So popular were these new spectacles that the management of the Foire Saint-Laurent theatre opened a new house called the Opéra - Comique, having obtained permission from the *Académie Royale de Musique* to introduce singers and musicians. Lesage and other well-known authors wrote plays for the new theatre, but the *Comédie française* instituted legal proceedings for infringement of their charter rights. The Opéra - Comique was therefore closed in 1718 and the fairs returned once more to their acrobatic and marionette shows. But meanwhile the wily Italians, back again in Paris,

old house, the Théâtre de l'Hôtel de Bourgogne, the drop-scene of which bore the challenging device: " Je renais." For a time, as we have seen, the troupe played in the summer months at the Foire Saint-Laurent, but with indifferent success. In town it drew fair audiences, who went to see comedies by Marivaux, de Boissy, and Saint-Foix, for the Italians now rarely played in their own tongue, which the new generation of the age of Louis XV would not learn. The success of Monet's Opéra-Comique was such, however, that the *Comédie italienne* requested permission to merge with the former mountebanks, and in 1762 the two spectacles became one which was henceforth known officially as the Théâtre Italien, though all Paris called it the Opéra-Comique. Comedy yielded to the more popular musical plays or *pièces à ariettes* on which Monet had built up his reputation. A schism took place in the troupe in 1789 and some of the seceding actors formed a new company called the Théâtre de Monsieur. The Revolution ruined their undertaking, as it did the Opéra-Comique, and in 1801 the elements were re-grouped to form the modern Opéra-Comique. It is interesting to note that the fair theatres, despite successive warnings and fines, were apparently incorrigible pirates, for we find in 1768 an *ordonnance* specially issued on their account. The troupes of acrobats and tight-rope walkers were reminded that they were given permission to play at the three fairs of Saint-Laurent, Saint-Germain, and Saint-Ovide solely in order "to procure to the people a recreation from its work and to distract it from the evil results which ensue from debauch and idleness." They were warned to discontinue their performances of plays belonging to the *Comédie française* and the *Comédie italienne* either "under their original or imaginary titles," of detached scenes from these plays or *parades* or *bouffonneries*, save by express permission. They were further ordered to limit their prices to three francs for the best seats, twenty-four sous for the second best, and twelve sous for the others, these being considered prices within the purse of the lower classes.

The French owe their opera to Italian influence, in particular to the initiative of Cardinal Mazarin who, in 1647, introduced Italian artists in *Orféo ed Euridice*, a three-act opera with elaborate scenic effects. It had an immediate success, though the public would have preferred a libretto in French. In the opinion of connoisseurs, however, French poetry was not adaptable to music, an absurd objection which Pierre Perrin disproved by writing a pastorale in five acts to the music of Cambert. This opera, though of indifferent quality and unaccompanied by ballets or scenic effects—*machines* as they were termed—was staged with tremendous success at Issy, to avoid, it is said, the overcrowding which would have occurred if it had been presented in Paris. This was in 1659, and from that moment the popularity of national opera was assured. Thanks to the genius of Lully, the composer, and the dramatic author, Quinault, French opera attained a high degree of perfection at the close of the seventeenth century.

Boileau, it is true, attempted to belittle the merit of Quinault, but as Boileau was hostile to any new form of art, his opinion in this matter, as in so many others, may be disregarded. The *Académie Royale de Musique* was now firmly established in the public favour and the French possessed what was really a conservatoire where training was given in singing, dancing, and music. A *concert spirituel* was also instituted for the benefit of lovers of sacred and liturgical music.

But after the death of Lully the *Opéra* was the object of a special royal *règlement* in which reference is made to indebtedness and a lack of discipline which threatened to deprive the public of this popular spectacle. The theatre was completely reorganised and, as a tonic to its financial debility, was granted the privilege of holding masked balls, and a dancing-floor was constructed by extending the stage over the parterre. Notwithstanding the rage for these notorious *bals de l'Opéra*, which were much frequented by the Regent and his dissolute friends, the *Opéra*, from 1712 to 1721, was administered by a committee of its creditors. All sorts of expedients were resorted to during the course of the century to wipe out its deficit, which had seemingly become chronic, but the fact was that Lully had left no real successor, so for the greater part of the eighteenth century French music was in a sorry pass despite the efforts of composers like Campra, Lacoste, and Bertin. The ballet suffered a similar decline, though the century produced some famous dancers, notably Dupré and Vestris. When,

towards the end of the reign of Louis XV, the vogue
for Italian music divided France into two violently
hostile camps, it was Italian music which eventually
won the day and the *Académie Royale de Musique*
had a hard struggle to keep its doors open. Many
thought, like the abbé Galiani, that it should be
moved out of town to Sèvres, opposite the bull-ring,
in accordance with the municipal regulation which
enacted that all loud noises must be kept outside the
city. Lack of discipline and of proper management
rather than a scarcity of talent seems to have been
the chief cause of the decline of the Paris opera.
The morals of the *filles d'Opéra* of this period are a
byword, and one has only to examine the secret
police reports of the century to see that it was not
ability as a singer or dancer which opened the golden
doors to success on the stage of the *Opéra*. The
actresses were almost without exception kept by
noblemen or financiers, who protected them against
the management, and even ladies of high rank vied
with each other in obtaining invitations to the private
boxes of these stars who used to visit the *Comédie
française* on the days when the *Opéra* was closed, for
only three performances a week were given at this
theatre. From all accounts the spectacle which
attracted audiences to the *Opéra* in the eighteenth
century was that which to-day appeals to the foreign
clientèle of the *Folies-Bergère*. Large sums were ex-
pended on costumes and scenery, and famous artists
like Boucher and Fragonard did not disdain to paint
for the *Opéra*. In addition, salaries accounted for a

respectable sum, since there were more than sixty
singers, about fifty dancers, and fifty instrumentalists.
The public was unwilling to pay the high prices for
entrance because for a third of the amount they could
hear Italian music at the Opéra-Comique and enjoy
better dancing, a genre in which the Italians of course
excelled. The *Opéra* frequently prosecuted both the
Comédie française and the *Comédie italienne*, though,
as we have seen, it sold to the Opéra-Comique permission to produce musical plays. In 1753 a dispute
arose with the *Théâtre français* which engaged some
Italian ballet-dancers rejected by the *Opéra*. The
House of Molière emerged victorious with the right
to give ballets on Mondays, Wednesdays, and Satur-
days, days when there was no performance at the
Opéra. In this case the *Comédiens du Roi* were
really at fault, a verdict having been pronounced
against them. But they closed their theatre as a
protest and petitioned Mme de Pompadour who requested the *prévôt des marchands*, then in charge of
the *Opéra*, to withdraw his complaint, which he
immediately did, since technically all playhouses
were the private perquisite of the King, being lent
to the public only as an act of royal favour. That
is why the other two theatres were administered by
the Gentlemen of the King's Bedchamber and were
included under the category of the *Menus Plaisirs
du Roi*. The *Opéra*, though sometimes under private
management, was farmed out in the same way as
was the collection of taxes.

Actors, or rather actresses, it is said, are difficult

people to manage. This was very true at all events
in the eighteenth century, when a special prison was
affected to the use of recalcitrant mummers, the
famous For l'Evêque, which formerly stood in the
Quai de la Mégisserie and whose history has been
so attractively related by M. Funck-Brentano in his
Bastille des Comédiens.

Now, the peculiar status of the actor under the old
regime placed him in a unique position in regard to
the law. By virtue of his calling he was automatically excommunicated by the Church and could
only approach the sacraments as an act of favour and
after petition. It was only with great difficulty, it
will be remembered, that permission could be obtained
to bury Molière according to the rites of the Catholic
Church, and even then the remains of the great playwright had to be smuggled to the grave by stealth,
and this at a time when the Archbishopric of Paris
was administered by a man who was a notorious
lecher. And yet the Church did not scorn to accept
a share of the receipts of the *Comédie française*. On
learning that the Capuchins were accorded a monthly
dole by the actors, the Cordeliers, *très-humblement*,
prayed to be placed on the list of the theatre's
charities in 1696 and, their request having been
granted, the Augustines of the Faubourg Saint-
Germain also tendered their very humble petition.
It is to be presumed that the money issuing from
such a polluted source underwent some sort of purifi-
cation at the hands of these spiritual alchemists. In
any case, the generosity of the actors was accepted

as a matter of course, and the ban was not lifted.
Originally the Church had been justified in her attitude, for there is no law, however iniquitous, which
was entirely so at its inception.   The mediaeval *far-
ceurs*, who first incurred ecclesiastical wrath, were a
godless crew and sorely in need of discipline, but
they bore as much resemblance to the *Comédiens du
Roi* as an African witch doctor does to a Harley Street
surgeon.   But the Catholic Church, like Montesquieu,
believed that one should rarely touch old-established
laws, or, at least, only "with trembling hand."   So
the following anomalous situation arose.   The public,
encouraged by clerical example, looked upon play-
actors as inferior beings, whilst the King, whose
servants they were, permitted a nobleman to act in
the *Comédie française* or in the *Opéra* without derogation to his nobility, thus defining the profession as
superior at least to that of commerce.   It is a moot
point as to whether an actor's evidence could be
accepted in an eighteenth-century French court of
law even under oath.   I think that the law in this
regard had been allowed to fall into abeyance, but
as in most cases the actor was dealt with by special
jurisprudence, it is difficult to find out what his
position was in the ordinary civil court.

The regulations governing the actor's relations with
the Gentlemen of the King's Bedchamber and his
situation in regard to authors and to the public are
clearly set forth in the annals of the *Comédie française*.
Essentially they are the same for the other State
theatres.   As we have noted, emoluments were liberal

and form the subject of elaborate legislation in which the actor's interests are carefully safeguarded. In addition to special perquisites when the troupe played at Court, every member of the company received a token worth six francs for attendance at the weekly general assemblies. On the other hand, absentees and late-comers were deprived of this *droit de présence* and there was a special scale of fines for such offences as not knowing one's part, missing a cue, failure to attend rehearsals, interrupting the deliberations of the assembly, or the use of indecorous language towards a colleague. Actors cast for a certain part had not the right to refuse it, and where illness was put forward as a reason for such conduct the *semainier* or chairman for the week had to satisfy himself that there was no malingering. Recidivists — and there were many—were handed over to the Gentlemen of the Bedchamber, who frequently sent such offenders to jail. Actors who refused to take small parts were fined three hundred francs and deprived of permission to play good ones, whilst in order to give beginners a fair chance, the regular members of the troupe were obliged, under pain of a fine of one hundred francs, to accept the rôles assigned to them by the *débutants* in the plays chosen by the latter. Admission to the three State theatres was then, as now, a high honour and new appointments were made only after a period of two years' probation. Before an actor was admitted or rejected, at the close of this period each member of the society had to send his verdict supported by his reasons to the *Intendant des Menus* who forwarded it to the Gentlemen of the Bedchamber.

Equally careful regulations governed the procedure to be observed in the choice of plays. Manuscript plays were read in a secret session of the assembly, at which the author replied to questions or objections raised by the actors. Up till 1766 the reading committee used to vote by secret ballot, blackballing unsuitable plays. After that date, however, each *sociétaire* had to put his or her objection in writing, and, significantly enough, the regulation stipulated that "Actors or actresses are forbidden to use any offensive language: they must expose their reasons clearly and in decent terms." The author cast his own play and the artists had to accept the parts allotted to them. For a five-act play the author received one-ninth of the net receipts, one-twelfth for a three-act piece, and one-eighteenth for a play of only one act. He could take his play off after a few performances, with the option of having it put in the repertory at a future time. However, if twice in succession or on any three occasions the takings fell below twelve hundred francs in winter or eight hundred in summer the play became the property of the actors, a regulation which opened the door to abuse, since it was in the interest of the theatre to "kill" a good play with the object of resurrecting it later when it became the property of the troupe. All through the century authors complained bitterly of this rule, and it is to the honour of Beaumarchais that after a long and determined fight he finally succeeded in obtaining for the playwright the same royalty privileges as other men of letters.

A famous incident reveals the situation of the actor in regard to the theatre public. A rather indifferent player, Dubois, refused to pay his doctor's bill, and the leech, as was customary, complained to the troupe. Mlle Clairon, the famous tragedienne, annoyed at the slight on her profession, communicated the affair to M. de Richelieu, Gentleman of the Bedchamber, who ordered the actors to try the case. As a result, Dubois, who was found guilty of perjury, was dismissed with the approval of the Gentlemen. But Dubois had a beautiful daughter, also an actress, whose charms so touched M. de Richelieu that he revoked the decision and ordered the actors to play with Dubois in the *Siège de Calais*. This was on 15 April, 1765, and on the morning of that day Le Kain, Clairon, and three other members of the cast handed in their parts. At the last minute it was resolved to substitute *Le Joueur* for the *Siège de Calais*. Meanwhile Mlle Dubois in the audience was busily moulding public opinion, and as she was young and very pretty the hotheads in the parterre ardently championed her cause. The curtain rose and Bouret, the *complimenteur* on that occasion, announced the change of programme. Immediately shouts arose of *Clairon au cabanon!* and for an hour the theatre resounded with curses, hissing, and booing. Some enthusiasts proposed setting fire to the building, and had the guards intervened, bloodshed would have resulted. In the end the management rang down the curtain and returned the entrance-money. The five members who refused to play were sent to For l'Evêque. Mlle Clairon, who acted off the stage as well as on it, made a speech in the grand Racinian manner to the police officer who was to take her to prison. "I submit to the King's orders," she declaimed. "Everything I have is at his Majesty's disposal—my property, my person, my life. But my honour must remain intact. The King himself has no claim on that." "Quite right!" retorted the officer, who had a dry sense of humour. "Where there is nothing the King loses his rights." Clairon's progress to For l'Evêque was a triumphal procession, and all fashionable Paris flocked to visit her. Meanwhile, one of the actors made a humble apology to the public on behalf of the troupe, expressing sincere repentance for having given offence and promising in future to try to merit the kindness and indulgence of the audience. The *Siège de Calais* was produced and the imprisoned players were released to act their parts and reincarcerated after the performance. Finally, owing to Clairon's influence, the affair was arranged as follows. The author withdrew his play for the time being and Dubois was pensioned off with a solatium of fifteen hundred francs and an annual bonus of five hundred francs for having trained his daughter as an actress. The prisoners were liberated after three weeks of enjoyable martyrdom and the comfortable reflection that they had scored a moral victory. It was most unusual for actors to be imprisoned for so long, since ordinarily a sojourn of a day or two was considered sufficient. Indeed, apart from the incident just narrated, where the public was, so to speak, the plaintiff, there were few serious cases. Occasionally a susceptible noble-man felt that his dignity had been offended by an actor, as for example the insufferable duc de Vismes, Gentleman of the Bedchamber, who had a dispute with Vestris the dancer. "Do you realise to whom you are talking?" inquired the irate Duke. "Yes. To the man who farms out my talent," replied the actor coolly. Sometimes a French artist, tempted by the promise of lucrative employment in England, deserted, and there is a case on record which shows that Garrick tried to recruit Parisian dancers through a certain Devisse of the *Opéra*. Temperamental singers who refused to play at the last moment, actors guilty of indecent "gagging," or of quarrelling or drunkenness on the stage, or of sitting too long over a bottle in the Café Procope and thus missing their cue, were all sent to For l'Evêque, but it is doubtful whether this punishment was looked on as anything more than an annoying contretemps by the majority of actors, though there were one or two who felt degraded by it. The popular artists, especially the women, realised that their talent made them practically immune, since they could always, like Clairon, threaten to resign if their requests were not granted. This famous actress did indeed retire at the height of her fame as a protest against the humiliations to which her profession was subjected by the public, and Mlle Lemaure, the Melba of the eighteenth century, imprisoned for having refused to give up a supper-party in order to play in *Jephté*, had her revenge by deserting the stage for the convent. Collé, who was a playwright and therefore inclined to be prejudiced against the "profession," asserts in 1771 that the actors were too well off and had become lazy, frequently sending their understudies because they were loath to leave their country houses in fine weather. Other writers, too, comment on the growing presumptuousness of the actor as the century advances, but although a few stars were indulgently tolerated by good society, the prejudice against the rank and file was maintained until the Revolution.

It is doubtful whether the actors of the present *Comédie française* intend to emulate their Anglo-Saxon colleagues by producing their great classic tragedies in modern dress. If, however, they do so they will simply be reverting to what was the regular practice of their predecessors in the eighteenth century. In the reign of Louis XIV an actress playing Phèdre or Iphigénie appeared in the ceremonial *habits de ville* of the day, though actors who represented ancient Greeks or Romans wore a costume consisting of a close-fitting tunic resembling a cuirass, a kilt such as Albanian or Greek peasants still affect, buskins, and flesh-coloured hose. Both men and women sported enormous head-dresses of ostrich feathers, though only in tragic rôles. In comedy ordinary street dress was the rule, and this of course varied with the caprice of the mode exactly as in our modern society plays. The Italians, however, had always possessed individual costumes for their traditional characters, Harlequin, Pantaloon, Pierrot, Scapin, Scaramouch, Columbine, and the Doctor. Some of these still survive in our modern pantomimes in the dress which they wore in the early eighteenth century. The Italians were very jealous of their "copyright," and when Riccoboni returned to France under the Regency he expressly stipulated that no other troupe in the country should be allowed to imitate either his characters or their costumes.

Adrienne Lecouvreur, whom Voltaire has immortalised in verses which vibrate with rare sensibility, abandoned town dress for the more magnificent Court robes of the period and in 1727 created something of a furore by appearing in Campistron's *Tiridate* in the exaggerated panniers of the day. About the same time the Roman warrior heroes discarded their pasteboard helmets for the more convenient small hats then in fashion, but did not give up their imposing nodding plumes. This strange conventional costume *à la romaine* was unique, as the usual practice both in comedy and in non-classical tragedy was to wear contemporary dress. For example, when Molière was produced in the eighteenth century, no attempt was made even to preserve the costumes of the time of Louis XIV. With a few notable exceptions such was the fashion which obtained until the Revolution. In the seventeenth century the *Opéra* had special fancy costumes of a purely arbitrary design, but under Louis XV this theatre followed

the example of the *Comédie française* and adopted
Court dress.   Were it not for the fact that no women
were allowed in the stage seats it might have been
conjectured that Mlle Lecouvreur's innovation was a
protective measure to prevent her from being confused with a crowd of inquisitive spectators.   As it
is, her adoption of the sumptuous and bejewelled
Court dress was probably merely a very feminine
desire to dazzle the *premières loges*.   Such was not
the case, however, with the actors who, in comedy
at least, must often have been indistinguishable from
the spectators on account of the similarity of attire.
This was not likely to be the case in classic tragedy
so long as the ostrich feathers and the traditional
"Roman" dress were retained.   As a matter of fact
the actors probably troubled very little about such
a trivial detail, since they had so many other and
more serious obstacles to contend with, like dogs,
drunken noblemen, and facetious interruptions from
the parterre.   On the whole, audience and players
were less interested in the costume and scenic effects
than in the acting and declamation.   Local colour
had not then become the obsession it now is, and it
struck everyone as the most natural thing in the world
that Horace should gravely put on his gloves, sheathe
his dagger, and gallantly assist Camille to her feet
when she tripped over her pannier.

But already in literature, particularly in the novel
and in comedy, writers were approaching more closely
to the external realities of life.   Voltaire in his *Mort
de César* dressed his senators in red robes, a daring

the same enterprising actress who first introduced genuine peasant costume on the stage in *Bastien et Bastienne*, where she created a sensation in the short skirt, straw hat, and *décolleté* corsage of the real country girl. Still, these were exceptions, and it was not really until the end of the century that Diderot's agitation for more realism began to make itself felt. Contrast, for example, the trouble taken by Beaumarchais in details regarding costume and *mise en scène* with the complete indifference of his predecessors, to whom this aspect of theatrical illusion meant little or nothing. A revolution was effected, however, in the art of stage decoration quite early in the century when Servandoni introduced the principle of oblique perspective on the stage of the *Opéra* which specialised in spectacular effects. Hitherto objects like temples, rocks, and trees had been shown in their entirety so that sometimes the actors towered above them. It was Servandoni who hit upon the plan of presenting them only in part, thus lending a suggestion of spaciousness which completely transformed the general picture. His reforms cost much labour and money and were thus not imitated by the other two houses, though Boucher, after Servandoni died, carried on his work at the *Opéra*. In the *Comédie française* the traditional setting for tragedy was the courtyard of a Roman palace or, to be more accurate, of a seventeenth-century private house, whilst comedy was played in an ordinary drawing-room setting. This was quite natural, for the preservation of the unity of place rendered a more elaborate scene almost impossible, though several private stages copied the ideas of Servandoni.

In the eighteenth century the mania for private theatricals possessed every class of society, as, according to the *Radoteur*, a magazine of the time, even peasants and artisans were smitten with the craze. "The mania is even spreading to the villages," we read. "Already we have acquired the habit of rising late, of devoting as few hours as possible to our affairs and the whole afternoon to our frivolities. It is a system which even the workmen are gradually adopting." Ironically enough, it was the Church which originated the vogue for play-acting. The Jesuits were ardent histrions and in all their colleges trained their pupils to take part in religious plays. Did not Racine salve his tormented conscience by writing *Athalie* and *Esther* for the pensionnaires of Mme de Maintenon's school at Saint-Cyr? Young girls acquired a taste for theatricals in their convent, and it is not surprising that after marriage they sought further opportunities to display their talents though, indeed, not in the type of play of which the good mother superior would have approved. Voltaire, as is well known, installed a theatre wherever he went and came into conflict with the Genevan Consistory, which regarded the theatre as the antechamber to hell and refused to allow actors in their city. He took parts in his own plays and, it is said, acted quite well, making up in enthusiasm for what he lacked in technique. One of his favourite rôles was that of the Christian patriarch Lusignan in *Zaïre*, and he must have presented a memorable spectacle as, with straggling locks and clenched fists raised to heaven, he declaimed the famous line, "Mon Dieu! j'ai combattu soixante ans pour ta gloire." One does not know whether the audiences derived as much pleasure from these productions as did Arouet himself. At any rate, according to an amusing anecdote, Montesquieu fell asleep in the middle of the *Orphelin de la Chine*, to the annoyance of the author, who threw his hat at the unappreciative spectator, crying, "Have you forgotten, Monsieur le Président, that you are no longer in the Law Courts?"

The duchesse du Maine, one of the supporters of Voltaire in his fight with Crébillon and the Pompadour cabal, owned a magnificent private theatre at Sceaux. Her tutor, Malézieu, who was as stage-struck as his pupil, was both author and producer, and, as M. Dubled points out in his fascinating book *La Comédie de Société*, this famous savant and member of the Academy did not scruple to write for the Sceaux theatre farces and *parades* of the most Rabelaisian nature. The members of the highest nobility loved these gross vaudevilles and frequently the reigning stars were required to give command performances of such *parades*, to the great delectation of Louis XVI and his aunts.

Mme de Pompadour, one of the most natural actresses of the eighteenth century, had a passion for private acting, but for her the theatre was a serious affair, where failure meant the loss of her position as titular mistress to the capricious and bored Louis XV. The theatre of the *Petits Cabinets* at Versailles became then the centre of Court intrigue, and a minor part in one of Mme de Pompadour's productions was often the first step to a high administrative post. The wily Voltaire, experienced sycophant though he was, fell from royal grace because of an ode in which he celebrated too indiscreetly the favourite's histrionic charms.

Louis XVI was not an enthusiastic lover of the theatre and, as we have seen, his taste in plays was low. Marie Antoinette, on the other hand, was passionately fond of acting and persuaded the reluctant Louis to allow her to install a theatre at Trianon. The Queen acted in light comedies, to the scandal of everyone, though the audience was limited to the King, his brother, and the royal princesses. Later, to encourage the players, a few servants were admitted, as being of no account, though the courtiers were rigorously excluded. By an odd coincidence the last stage appearance of this unhappy lady was in the part of Rosine in Beaumarchais's *Le Barbier de Séville*, that joyous comedy which conceals beneath the bubbling froth of its laughter the acid dregs of a satire directed against contemporary society.

THE CENSORSHIP

One of the few privileges retained by the University of Paris is that of granting permission to print doctoral theses. But the privilege is merely a nominal, or at least a local one, for the *Recteur*, when he appends the magic words *Vu et approuvé* to the manuscripts submitted by aspiring doctors of letters, is simply indicating that the works in question have a reasonable chance of passing the jury of professors who are to pronounce on their value as original contributions to literature. But in the old days, when the Sorbonne was a city within a city, armed with all the authority which the mediaeval Church could bring to bear upon her recalcitrant children, the *Recteur's* veto was an absolute decree which no author dared flout save at his bodily and spiritual peril.

Before the days of printing, books passed through many hands before reaching the public. A *parche-minier* prepared the skins for the vellum used by the author, a lengthy if not a complicated process. The book was then most probably submitted to the *libraire* who combined the functions of bookseller and publisher. It was he who decided whether the work was saleable enough to warrant the expense of illustration and copying. The beautiful art of illuminating the manuscript was carried out by an *enlumineur* who decorated the initial letter of each chapter with *or bruni* and in the case of expensive books with those gorgeous reds and blues which to this day have preserved the primitive splendour of their tints. Closely associated with the *libraires* were the *écrivains* or copyists who performed the rôle now played by the printer and who, it is interesting to note, were originally called *stationnaires*, or stationers, because they carried out their business in certain fixed places.

As early as the thirteenth century the University exercised a sort of control over sellers and publishers of books. Such *libraires* were obliged to appear, preferably every year, but in any case every two years, before the assembled Faculty of Theology of the Sorbonne to swear that they would conduct themselves loyally in the exercise of their business. They might not sell on their own account books entrusted to them for deposit until such works had been exposed for at least a month. To protect the author against trickery, all books had to be placed where they could easily be seen by the public, with the title and price clearly marked. Further, the price of the book had to be paid direct to the author or owner, though the bookseller was allowed the fairly liberal profit of twenty-five per cent. Booksellers who broke these regulations were deprived of their office and instructions were issued to all students and masters to have no dealings with them. This of course spelled ruin, because all the book trade was centred round the University colleges and abbeys, whilst, apart from the loss of sales, the *libraires* had to give up the very profitable business of lending books in return for a sum, also fixed by the omnipotent *Recteur*.

But alas! in those days even publishers were apparently incorrigibly dishonest, for in the fourteenth century we find the Sorbonne obliged to issue new regulations in order to check malpractices. Persons desiring to engage in the book trade were now required to produce credentials and to pay a fee of one hundred francs for their *lettres*, i.e. the permission to trade accorded by the *Recteur*. They were also bound to inform the University before disposing of a book, in case the volume might be required for the library of the Sorbonne. Again, in order to protect students, the *Recteur* ordered the *libraire* to submit to his inspection such books as he intended to hire out. This very necessary precaution was designed to ensure that the student should obtain the pure text and, where the copyist had been careless, the masters of the Sorbonne insisted on a corrected edition. The subscription fees for lending libraries were lowered and a maximum price was fixed for the copying of manuscripts, with the further injunction that the *libraire* could not refuse permission to copy any book in his possession. The number of *libraires* was limited to twenty-eight, though there was no lack of applicants for licences to sell and publish.

The invention of printing gave rise of course to several changes in the book business. The first French printing-press was installed in the "maison de la Sorbonne" in 1470, but operated slowly. Thus in 1471 we find Louis XI borrowing from the Faculty of Medicine the copy of a treatise by an Arabian physician. The University, in return for twelve gold marks and a deposit of one hundred golden crowns, graciously lent the volume, "all this out of great obedience and zeal to please the King." As printed books became more common a crisis arose in the printing trade about the end of the fifteenth century when, owing to the lack of proper control, large numbers of badly printed and pirated works flooded the markets, resulting in the ruin of many printers. Erasmus first conceived the idea of appealing to the Sovereign, and limited monopolies or *privilèges*, usually for not more than two years, were accorded for certain books. At this stage it was very rare to find new books printed. The manuscripts which went to press were as a rule nobody's property, the author being unknown or long dead. The great printing centre in those days was not Paris but Lyons, which retained its supremacy as a publishing centre until the beginning of the seventeenth century.

Publishers and printers seem to have amalgamated early in the sixteenth century because a University regulation of 1517 forbade them conjointly to print or sell the *Concordat*, and it is certain that by 1538 the two trades were firmly established in Paris as a joint community with twelve to fourteen presses employing two hundred and fifty workmen and consuming two hundred reams of paper a week. It was about this time, too, that some attempt was made to regularise the question of censorship and monopolies. François I by letters patent in 1541 commanded that all books dealing with religious questions should be approved by the Faculty of Theology of Paris before going to press, whilst Henri II, doubtless at the instance of the University, forbade the printing of any books of an anti-religious nature under pain of confiscation of "body and property." Also, the name of the printer, of the author, and of the place of printing had to appear on the title-page of all published books.

In 1560 there are indications that the University is beginning to lose some of her privileges, for we hear of certain printers engaged in the publication of *libelles* or pamphlets with the authorisation of the King but without having taken the usual oath before the Faculty. It seems that now the Government, realising the political importance of the community of printers and publishers, resolved to take under its control the whole business of the writing, printing, and publishing of books, or, as it was collectively designated, the *Librairie*. But the University did not lose its power of veto entirely, particularly, of course, in the case of works dealing with religious questions, on which the Sorbonne was obviously most competent to pronounce an opinion. To show that it was taking its self-imposed duties seriously, the Government, in 1560, hanged a publisher who was discovered with copies of a certain pamphlet against the Guises and the University; and two years later, issued a number of decrees regarding *libraires* on the occasion of the religious troubles. An ordinance issued in 1561 by the Parlement or Supreme Court of Paris forbade the printing of any work without the permission of King or Parlement and took vigorous action to suppress the publication of lampoons in a somewhat badly worded and ambiguous decree of 1563, from which one gathers that not only printers of libellous pamphlets but also of books without permission were liable to the death penalty. Later decrees, however, make it clear that only the former were put to death, whereas the latter got off with fines and corporal punishment. During this period of internecine strife, the Huguenots in particular evaded the obligatory visit to the University, and the Parlement ordered that all works on the "so-called reformed religion" should be submitted for approval to the Parlements of the provinces. The University meanwhile had not been idle, having already obtained permission to forbid the printing of any books attacking the "sound religion," though it is significant that this veto did not apply to Paris and its suburbs.

In spite of this accumulation of regulations, or rather because of it, Government control of the *Librairie* was far from effective and, whilst contraband literature in France itself was kept within reasonable proportions, little check could be kept on the publication of such literature in adjacent countries. The threat of confiscation and of a fine of four thousand crowns did little to suppress this new development in the illicit book trade, whilst new

problems in connection with the granting of monopolies or *privilèges* added to the embarrassment of
French officialdom.

By the end of the sixteenth century the *communauté*
of printers and publishers had apparently become a
powerful guild, jealous of its rights. In 1572,
through their syndics, they raised the whole question
of privileges, taking as a test case the monopoly
granted to one Kewer for the printing of breviaries,
missals, and other books of devotion. Holding that
to accord such absolute monopolies was prejudicial
to free trade and the public weal, they suggested
that privileges of this kind should be granted only
where the printer or publisher had incurred expenses
either in the payment of authors' fees or by disburse-
ments to specialised proof-readers called in to correct
a defective manuscript. Here again it is significant
that the University sided with the *Librairie* and, in
1582, the *Recteur* was instrumental in obtaining for
Paris a privilege which had been accorded at first
exclusively to Lyons. In view of later developments
in the eighteenth century it is amusing to contemplate
this attitude.

The general situation about the beginning of the
eighteenth century was that no printer or publisher
could get a book printed or reprinted without having
previously obtained permission in the form of *lettres
scellées du grand sceau*, and right up to the Revolution
it was the Keeper of the Seals who was, nominally
at any rate, the supreme authority in all matters
even remotely connected with the world of books.

The case of Antoinette Carteron in 1704 reveals the severity with which the above regulation was enforced. For printing the *Praticien français* without permission this woman lost her licence. Her printing-press and type were confiscated and, as was the custom, sold in the chamber of the Guild of Printers and Publishers. The money thus obtained went to the hospitals. The sheets were seized and crushed to pulp in the *pilon*, a machine used for this special purpose. But this was not all. Her employees were declared incapable of ever becoming master printers and forbidden to work under any master printer in the capacity of journeymen in any town in the kingdom. Another offender, the widow Baujolin, in consideration of her situation, was only fined three *livres*, but her employees were mulcted of fifty and one hundred *livres* respectively.

From one point of view the history of eighteenth-century France may be regarded as the account of a long and bitter struggle for the freedom to write. There is in the *Bibliothèque Nationale* the manuscript of a scheme "to establish a council for the furtherance of literature and the encouragement of savants." It was never, I believe, put into effect, but it is clear from the suggestions put forward that authors were in many cases the victims of stupidity, ignorance, and prejudice. Many of the censors, we learn, lacked that "age, penetration, prudence, and erudition" requisite in men of their calling. Others, it is bluntly stated, especially in the department of theology, were looked upon by the public as the tools of other secret censors whose religious prejudices they shared.

From the mass of documents preserved in the above library it is possible to form a fairly clear impression of the working of the complicated machinery devised by the Government to control the *Librairie*.   By the eighteenth century this task of supervision was an extremely difficult one, since it entailed keeping watch on everyone connected with literature, from the author down to the street hawker or *colporteur*, and, what was more awkward, it meant placating courtiers and other influential people who were interested either in suppressing or protecting an author for personal reasons.   Usually the Keeper of the Great Seal appointed a director who worked in close liaison with the Lieutenant-General of Police, a gentleman whose shadow lies athwart the whole history of the century. The direct supervision was entrusted to inspectors who, like most highly-placed functionaries of the time, purchased their position or *charge*.   The actual salary which they received, eight hundred francs, represented a return of four per cent on their capital outlay, and in addition the inspector drew twenty-five francs when he accompanied the Commissioner of Police on judicial inquiries, fifty francs from the Crown for every conviction, and a hundred francs when, at the request of a parent, he imprisoned a member of a family.   This last item seems surprising till we remember that these inspectors were not exclusively concerned with the *Librairie*.   Some, for example, looked after money-lenders, gambling, prostitutes, and indeed any police matters which happened to arise in their districts. In addition to these permanent inspectors there were a great many auxiliaries used for special cases and who, besides tracking down clandestine printers, frequented inns, theatres, and other public resorts, keeping their ears open for odds and ends of gossip concerning men in political or administrative posts. They seem to correspond fairly closely to the inspectors of the present-day *police secrète*.

Until about 1737 the syndics of the Guild of Printers and Publishers enjoyed the confidence of the Government, with whom they co-operated as follows. Books arriving at the Port of Paris were deposited in the chamber of the syndics, who were obliged to examine them every Tuesday and Friday before granting permission to put them on the market. The examination, however, appears to have become a mere formality, and Hérault, then Lieutenant-General of Police, dismissed some of the syndics and seized the opportunity to appoint an inspector of police whose duty was really to supervise the syndics. The latter, always jealous of their rights, objected strenuously to the innovation, which they regarded as an insult, but Hérault, though apparently anxious to placate them, sent one de Beauchamps to carry out the new duties. His letter to the syndics has been preserved and throws an interesting light on the relations existing between the *Librairie* and the Government.

Do not be pained or surprised [he writes] at the appointment of this inspector. If the *Librairie* had always been in such competent and faithful hands as yours, and if one could hope that your successors might resemble you, His Majesty would Himself have considered the precaution which He is taking as quite superfluous, but you know what has happened and you cannot be unaware of the grounds for fear which the future may hold in store. . . .

De Beauchamps seems to have been, unfortunately, tactless and stupid, if not actually dishonest. The syndics accused him of inventing charges so as to justify his appointment, and when, in 1750, Malesherbes was made director of the *Librairie*, a vigorous effort was made to prejudice him against de Beauchamps. The syndics pointed out that they were bound by oath to supervise printers and publishers, a fact which made the presence of an inspector offensive and equivocal. They accused de Beauchamps of unpunctuality. The visits began at 3 p.m., and the inspector, it seems, after having enjoyed a copious meal, arrived when the examination was nearly over. His practice was to sleep off the effects of his libations in the chamber of the syndics and then, waking with a bad headache and in a vile temper, he used to rate the officials of the *Librairie*, "using rude, obscene, violent, and absolutely inexcusable language in an office where order and decency should always accompany the functions which these officers exercise in the public service." He was accused, too, of venality in selling his protection to publishers of forbidden books and also of slackness in the execution of his duties, which he sometimes neglected for four months at a time. He was retired in 1757 on the grounds of old age.

But de Beauchamps was an exception. An excellent type of inspector was one of his successors, d'Hémery, who finally became chief inspector under the directorship of Malesherbes. Under the joint direction of these two able men the *Librairie* was wisely controlled during a great part of the eighteenth century. D'Hémery was a born organiser and, indeed, he had no sinecure. He was inspector of ports, a position which he held by virtue of a decree of the council; the Lieutenant-General of Police entrusted him also with the supervision of all printers, publishers, and street booksellers. Finally, he carried out with as much success as one could expect the unpopular duties so badly handled by de Beauchamps. But, paragon though he was, not even a d'Hémery could avoid falling foul of the *Librairie*.

In 1758, d'Hémery, in the interests not only of the police but of the publishers themselves, asked Malesherbes for authority to make domiciliary visits in order to arrest the owners of clandestine presses. He was very conscious of the apathy of the syndics and, to mitigate as far as possible the evil results of their slackness, he further proposed to inspect all printing-works and to require from all type-founders a periodical statement of the amount of metal they consumed, together with a declaration of its destination. Through their syndics, the printers and publishers protested vehemently to Malesherbes, who met all their objections with suave and sensible replies.

It is interesting to follow in the correspondence of Malesherbes the progress of this long and sturdily contested duel.

In reply to a complaint that the honour of the syndics had been impugned the director pointed out how impossible it was for them, in view of the important nature of their regular business, to give that time and thought to the bi-weekly examinations which the seriousness of such a task demanded, unless they received that assistance from the police which was now offered. The syndics replied that their domicile was inviolable, to which Malesherbes retorted that all merchants and tradesmen whose goods were susceptible of contraband had long been accustomed to such inspection and that for the *libraires* to continue to enjoy immunity was grossly unfair. The *communauté* now fell back on another line of defence and cited cases where, they alleged, the courts had opposed the institution of domiciliary visits to manufacturers of playing-cards, even though such visits were to be made only on warrant. Malesherbes' reply was a flat contradiction. He added that the syndics did not know what they were talking about. Some manufacturers of playing-cards were liable to visit without warrant. But still the battle went on. The majority of printers and publishers were installed in premises belonging either to colleges or convents, and such constant police inspections, they said, would be sure to annoy the landlords, who might refuse to renew their leases. The indefatigable director was ready for them. "A bad and insincere reason," was his comment. Why, he pursued, should the colleges and convents object to the visits of the inspectors any more than to those of the syndics, which presumably have been regularly carried out? There might be some reason for regarding these visits as an inquisition, he added, if they were made in private houses on the pretext of a search for clandestine presses. But many publishers, said the desperate syndics, were afraid that the inspectors might abuse their powers in order to exact moneys in return for protection. Malesherbes' stern reply was a demand for the names of such publishers, whom he threatened with the severest punishment for defaming the character of Government officials. The honours of the day were his, but his opponents were by no means silenced.

One gathers, then, that the post of Director of the *Librairie* was not a bed of roses. And, from a request submitted by the inspector-general, d'Hémery, in 1773, to be relieved of certain of his duties, we get some slight idea of the responsibility and burden of work attaching to this post, even allowing for the fact that d'Hémery was an exceptionally gifted and experienced official. Here is an abbreviated list of his functions: the supervision of authors, printers, publishers, and booksellers; the search for clandestine presses and for books printed without permission; the handling of complaints; the supervision of lotteries of street hawkers, books, and prints; arrests; inspection of public writers and the collection of specimens of their handwriting; replies to anonymous letters;

statistics regarding apprentices, journeymen, and master printers. Is it surprising that after some sixteen years of this work he should ask for the appointment of an additional inspector? One is relieved to be able to say that his request was granted.

The tussle between Malesherbes and the syndics is a mere incident in a long and hereditary feud which was fought round the burning question of monopolies or *privilèges*. Originally privileges were asked for only for old books. Later they were granted to publishers of recent works but for a limited period, and authors or their relatives used to have such privileges renewed so that a book came to be regarded as property which, like real estate, could be willed from one generation to another. But from the point of view of the public such renewals were looked upon as unfair, and there is no doubt that they constituted an abuse in the eyes of publishers who were unfortunate enough not to possess privileges for saleable books.

The Chancellor Seguier, in the sixteenth century, permitted renewals for modern books but not for old ones. Opposition arose from certain publishers, but as they were mostly small tradesmen doing business on the Pont-Neuf or at street corners, their protests were disregarded by Seguier, though it is fairly clear that the University was behind them. Finally, Étienne, the most influential printer in Paris, stated openly his opinion, which was that the Chancellor's scheme would help to suppress piracy in the trade, and so the situation calmed down. However, though

it was a perfectly well-established fact that "old"
books meant books written before the invention of
printing, several publishers and printers, feigning
ignorance, produced editions of modern works in
defiance of Seguier's regulations. Thus, for example,
someone printed the works of Saint François de Sales,
the monopoly for which had been given to another.
This necessitated a special decree in 1671 defining
the term *anciens livres*. On the Chancellor's death,
in 1671, determined and repeated attempts were
made to undo his work, but his successors, d'Aligres
and Le Tellier, were adamant. What happened,
indeed, was that the decree was registered in 1686
and so became permanent.

Yet, as time went on, the Crown began to doubt
the equity of its own regulations and to question the
advisability of granting perpetual renewals. It also
saw in the *Librairie* a profitable source of revenue
at a time—in 1777 to be exact—when the financial
situation was giving cause for grave anxiety. The
result of the deliberations of the council governing
the *Librairie* appeared in the form of new articles
of a revolutionary sort. A fresh scale of fees for
ordinary permission to print was evolved. No tax
was imposed for classic authors, but for modern
books the charges were as follows:

Format					Each volume of 1500 copies
in 32mo	.	.	.	.	30 sous
in 24mo	.	.	.	.	3 francs 15 sous
in 18mo	.	.	.	.	7 francs 10 sous
in 16mo	.	.	.	.	15 francs

Format				Each volume of 1500 copies
in 12mo	.	.	.	. 30 francs
in 8vo	.	.	.	. 60 francs
in 4to	.	.	.	. 120 francs
in folio	.	.	.	. 240 francs

The various towns in France were classified into four categories for the purpose of assessing the fees to be paid by persons desirous of going into business either as publishers or as printer-publishers. Paris, with its suburbs, was treated as a first-class town, and here the scale was as follows. The son of a master printer desiring to engage in publishing only, paid twelve hundred francs, and if he wanted a licence to set up as a printer, he paid an additional seven hundred. The son-in-law of a master paid thirteen hundred or two thousand francs, and apprentices the much higher fees of two thousand, or three thousand if they wished to become printers also. These regulations were irksome to some, but obviously not to the old-established printer-publishers. But the *libraires* or publishers were now for the first time established as a definite corps and this gave rise to discontent, particularly in the small provincial towns where the *libraire* was ordinarily a bookseller, i.e. a *libraire* in the modern sense of the term. Numbers of such small tradesmen, many of whom lived from hand to mouth, envisaged the future with anxiety. Where were they to find the money to pay the fees now necessary to set up their sons in business? The wiser members of the *Librairie*, too, foresaw an increase in the number of clandestine publishers who, they said, could evade the regulations by setting up as *éditeurs*, *commis d'auteurs*, *banquiers de librairie*, under which evasive titles they could continue to publish in defiance of the law.

So far, then, the Crown was faced only with the usual grumbling which greets every administrative innovation. The real storm broke on the publication of the articles dealing with *privilèges*. It was no longer possible to renew monopolies automatically, and such monopolies were henceforth to be granted for ten years or during the lifetime of the author. On the death of an author, or at the expiration of a privilege, the permission to reprint was thrown open to competition. Further, every author who had a permission to print could sell his works at his own house and, if he had not sold his rights to a publisher, his book was his property and could be handed down to his heirs *à perpétuité*. A flood of petitions poured in. The syndics of the printer-publishers, instead of going to the Parlement, appealed to the Keeper of the Seal. The *Recteur* of the University added his protests. The King was approached, but in vain. So the printers and publishers retired, sullen but expectant, adopting for the time being what they described as an attitude of "passive but respectful resistance."

Some idea may be formed of the grievances and undoubted hardships incurred by the publishers from the *Mémoire* of the *sieur* Leclerc which begins:

Like all the Paris publishers, I do not possess the right to print any book or part thereof save by acquisition. The source of the greater part of my property is the acquisition which I made of my father's capital by an agreement signed before my lawyer, Dulion, on 27 January, 1758, an acquisition the half of which I paid over to my sister.

After detailing the various items which he possesses, either as his father's heir, as author, or as acquisitor, he exposes his deplorable situation:

I am fifty-four. I maintain a wife and five children, the survivors of a family of fourteen. My necessary household expenses prevent me from increasing my patrimony though I spend nothing on amusement. In spite of my lack of fortune, the esteem in which I am held by my comrades has enabled me to occupy all the positions which a man in my condition may aspire to and in which, I venture to say, I have performed some service. If I have to lose my publishing capital, the only thing which I possess in the world, I should regard as a blessing the death of a sixth child whom I have lost since the publication of the decree of last August. I do not desire the death of the others, but I should regard my own with equanimity, so as not to be a witness of the misery in store for my children. But I am reassured by the kindness and righteousness of the King, who will not deprive me of my property which I acquired on the faith of the laws then in force.

A crop of lawsuits resulted from the new regulations. Here is a case which illustrates the difficulties confronting the administration of the *Librairie*. A month before the appearance of the new ordinances, an author sold his manuscript to a publisher who, of course, as the law then ran, acquired it in perpetuity. But by the new law he acquired it only till the author's death, or for ten years were the author to die before that period. The publisher refused to print the book and was sued by the vendor who was advised to obtain a new permission according to the new regulations. The publisher appealed and was granted perpetual possession of the manuscript, whilst a counter-appeal by the author was quashed. The decree of the council of the *Librairie* was therefore not recognised by the courts.

Nobody was content. The authors, who might have been supposed to be so, were annoyed because where they had formerly been accustomed to look on their work as their undisputed property they were now given to understand that they were proprietors only as an act of grace on the part of the Crown. The printers and publishers saw their perpetual possession reduced to a very limited period and the journeymen printers complained loudly at the exorbitant fees and irksome formalities required by the authorities. The latter replied that a great part of the moneys obtained from such fees would be repaid to the employees in the form of various grants for sickness, disablement, and, after thirty years' service, of pensions. As this system had long been in vogue, these arguments had not that glitter of novelty which in such cases can alone still the murmurings of a proletariat. The object of the new regulations regarding *privilèges*, as the Crown pointed out, was to protect the public, the author, and the publisher. It was only just that the first should have more extensive rights than the second. The old system was unjust to the public which had to pay high prices because of the monopolies which, moreover, encouraged piracy and prevented healthy competition.

But the printers and publishers, many of whom were faced with ruin, retorted that unlimited competition, whilst useful in other branches of commerce, was a source of evil in the publishing trade. There is a limit to the supply of other commodities but not to books. As a result of such unlimited competition, printers and publishers were amassing large stocks which they would never dispose of, and, in their haste to outdo one another, many were printing badly, which was leading to a general decay in the art of typography. Again, was the author really going to benefit from the new regulations? He could now, of course, undertake an edition of his works at his own expense, but what chance had a tyro in the highly specialised business of printing and publishing? If, on the other hand, he sold his manuscript to a publisher, he could not expect under the new conditions an offer which would recompense him for his expenditure of time and energy. Besides, said the *Librairie*, to accord preferential and paternal treatment to authors was nonsense, as if authors were not capable of entering into business contracts on their own account! The new scheme was a direct incentive to venality on the part of those responsible for disposing of the new privileges on the expiry of the old ones. Theoretically, the monopoly went to the highest bidder: would this really be so in practice? The *Librairie* very much doubted it. Again, the new rules would mean the disappearance of useful and serious works, as illustrated by the cases of Brillon's *Dictionnaire des Arrêts* and Ricardo's *Traité des Donations*. The monopoly for each of these works, the sale of which was very slow, was acquired under the old system by a syndicate of publishers who invested a great deal of capital in the venture. These syndicates were now to lose their money and, of course, would in future print only quick-selling, popular books which promised an immediate return for their capital outlay. The publishers suggested a compromise and asked that the new regulations be not made retroactive, or that at least a transition period be arranged to allow them to get rid of their stocks, but the Chancellor stood firm. So the unpopular regulations remained.

We have seen that under the old regime no book could be printed without a permit, which was granted by the *Chancelier*,[1] as nominal head of the censorship (in reality by the director), if the report of the censor was satisfactory. This *approbation* was granted only when the censor had assured himself that the work in question contained nothing detrimental to religion, to the King's authority, or to morality. During the second half of the eighteenth century, when the intellectual revolution headed by Voltaire and the Encyclopædists was at its height, the censors had a very unenviable task, for, if they were held up to ridicule on the one hand by the *philosophes* when their judgments erred on the side of too much prudence,

---

[1] Who was usually also *garde des sceaux*.

they were, on the other, liable to imprisonment if they failed to carry out their duties to the satisfaction of the authorities. A certain Coqueley de Chausse-pierre, for instance, was imprisoned at Vincennes for having approved of a book by the abbé Coyer which the Chancellor afterwards judged subversive of the authority of the Crown. Similarly, in 1757, a Bou-logne censor called Marteau was exiled to Montreuil for his excess of zeal in attacking a work favourable to the Unigenitus Bull. The censors were themselves the object of supervision, and a secret report exists, addressed apparently to Malesherbes, from which it seems that most of the censors were far from im-partial, particularly in regard to religious works. For convenience, censors were divided into four classes—theology, jurisprudence, natural history, and *belles lettres*, and, if we believe the confidential report, the last category contained a large number of ignoramuses who asked for the work either because it might be a stepping-stone to something better or in the hope that it might lead to a pension. The office was, however, not a sinecure. Every page of the book to be examined had to be read, initialled, and returned with a somewhat lengthy résumé indicating the offend-ing passages, with reasons for objection. Many of the reports are extraordinarily like modern book reviews and discuss such matters as style, presenta-tion of ideas, and the moral character of the author. Frequently certain passages were changed or sup-pressed. A typical example is afforded by the French translation of the *Letters* of Lord Chesterfield where "sous le despotisme de Louis XIV" is altered to "sous l'autorité absolue de Louis XIV," and for the phrase "Richelieu vint qui enchaîna la nation, Mazarin et Louis XIV rivèrent les clous des fers qu'on lui avait donnés," there was substituted "Richelieu vint qui travailla à élever l'autorité royale au plus haut point: Mazarin et Louis XIV achevèrent ce que Richelieu avait commencé," which is of course exactly the opposite of what Chesterfield intended to convey. Sometimes a publisher, either through inadvertence or intentionally, forgot to incorporate such changes stipulated by the censor, and in these cases a *carton* had to be inserted correcting the error. Before receiving permission to print, the publisher was obliged to give a signed undertaking that he would insert such *cartons* or corrections.

Censorship was obligatory for books of every sort, even for scientific or medical works, which were carefully scrutinised. For instance, in the translation of a certain English medical treatise the statement appeared that arsenic should be used internally for epilepsy, and the work was granted an *approbation* only on condition that a *carton* be inserted contradicting this statement. Often, too, the censor, whilst approving the views expressed by the author, refused permission to print for fear of international complications, as happened once or twice in 1778 during the strained relations with England. Of course, the censor's approval was not final and often he shrank from the responsibility of pronouncing a verdict, submitting the matter in such cases to the Keeper of the Seals, the *Garde des Sceaux*, though the last word was actually pronounced by the director of the *Librairie*. Usually books appeared with the *privilège* printed on the last page and embodying the censor's report, which was often a useful form of advertising. But sometimes no *approbation* was given and the book then appeared armed with a "tacit permission," which seems to have amounted to a mere verbal assurance on the part of the administration that they would connive at publication, but quite unofficially, since they promised no protection in case of trouble. One author, for example, had sent a copy of his book to the *Garde des Sceaux* and had received a letter of thanks which he interpreted as a *permission tacite*. The syndics, however, refused to allow the book to circulate until the administration of the *Librairie* expressed themselves more definitely. On the whole, the censorship was not a success. Many of its officers were indifferent; others were prejudiced and undoubtedly used their position to satisfy private grudges. Others, again, were incompetent to pronounce on the works submitted. But the chief objection to the system was the impossibility of closing the frontier against the floods of contraband books in French which were printed in England, Germany, Switzerland, and the Netherlands, and the public entered with zest into the game of hoodwinking the authorities by paying large sums to itinerant hawkers for forbidden works which were coveted by men about town and read aloud in fashionable *salons*.

dismissing a man without eight days' notice. Cadou had no difficulty in getting a post even without his clearance certificate, which masters very seldom demanded. But Simon who, if we believe Cadou, was a very vindictive man, informed the chamber of syndics of the irregularity. Cadou was now obliged to ask for his *billet de sortie*, since a circular letter had been sent to all master printers on the subject. Not unnaturally there was a violent scene in which, says Cadou, he was greeted with "humiliating apostrophes." The workmen printers clubbed together to enable their comrade to sue Simon, who was summoned to produce the clearance certificate. But in the meantime Simon had gone to the police with alarmist stories of a general revolt of workmen, and these seemed to be corroborated by the publication of Cadou's summons. A verbal order was issued to arrest the ex-employee and he was placed in solitary confinement for eleven days without being questioned and, after five days' further imprisonment, was released with the advice to go to Simon and apologise. But instead of doing this Cadou made a triumphal round of visits to the various printing-houses, stirring up the workmen who came out on strike and organised collections for legal expenses. The upshot was that Simon was sentenced to hand over the clearance certificate and to pay damages, a verdict pronounced, not by the administration of the *Librairie*, but by the courts, which did not always support the former and frequently, for example, prosecuted authors who had been granted a privilege by the censorship.

Such, very briefly, was the general working of the Government control of books under the monarchy, and though it was revived fitfully during the early nineteenth century, particularly under Napoleon, it never really survived the blow aimed at it by the National Assembly at the outbreak of the Revolution. Like all prohibitive legislation, it was good in so far as it curbed licentiousness, but we have only to read some of the productions of the early eighteenth century to realise how very indulgent the censorship was towards immorality. Its chief *raison d'être* was political, and here, judging from the achievements of the *philosophes*, it appears to have been singularly inefficient. On the other hand, the existence of a censorship made it impossible for all but the very wealthy to obtain "subversive" works so that, quite apart from other reasons, the propaganda of the *philosophes*, who were monarchists, was not a direct cause of the Revolution. They were chiefly influential in converting the enlightened section of the nobility and bourgeoisie to their ideas. This fact is reflected in the programmes of reform submitted to the King between 1781 and 1785 by his ministers: Calonne, Necker, Loménie de Brienne and others.